Men are not made for safe havens.

—Robert F. Kennedy, June 2, 1968

The Urban Guerrilla

THE URBAN

GUERRILLA

by Martin Oppenheimer

Chicago: Quadrangle Books

Library of Congress Catalog Card Number: 69-20159

Second Printing and first Quadrangle Paperback edition
published 1970.

For the members of the Columbia Commune,

April 1968

CONTENTS

The Urban Guerrilla

This book was conceived several days after the assassination of Reverend Martin Luther King, Jr., in April 1968. Although based on some work done earlier, the actual text was begun on June 6, 1968, the day that Senator Robert F. Kennedy died of an assassin's bullet. In a way, this book marks the end of one portion of a sociologist's career, that part having to do with the ongoing study of and participation in what was known as the civil rights movement of the 1960's. That movement, characterized by a devotion to the fulfillment of the "American Dream," to nonviolence, and to integration, seems now to be over. It foundered on the rock of society's resistance to the social changes needed to accomplish that dream. It is trite to suggest once again that race relations in this country are at a crossroads, yet this book is to a large degree a product, and somewhat less directly a discussion, of that crossroads.

The roads seem to me now to number three; they can be analyzed, I think, in terms of "establishment strategies," that is, in terms of how the American power structure may proceed. One is the road of repression, of creating a police state in the face of increasingly dangerous social movements and demands for change. The second is that of integrationist reform, and represents a continuation of present policies to try to solve the "race relations" situation by means of opening up certain levels of society to members of minority groups. A third and relatively newer road is that of establishment support for some "black power," a development which I shall refer to later on as "neo-colonialism." The first road, of repression, means race war between the armed representatives of government and those black people who see only violence left as a response to a desperate attempt to wipe them out as a people. Integrationist reform means continuing stagnation as the political and social obstacles to a really open society continue to block that kind of solution. Supporting some "black power" means black survival as a colony within white society; it is not a solution.

These particular roads, like so many things in sociology, are "ideal types," that is, they are extremes for the purpose of illustration. Reality at any given moment approximates some combination of these roads and varying stages along them. What we see is no clear way ahead but a muddling-through, as our society and its establishment try fumblingly to develop a strategy to cope with crisis after crisis, both domestic and international, without in any real way being able to *solve* those crises.

These visible roads, then, try to manage an increasingly oppressive situation without basically altering the status quo. The alternative to them is revolution—violent, nonviolent, or both—involving a radical movement of both black and white fundamentally to reconstruct American society. This alternative lies beyond the three roads I have just briefly outlined, for revolution comes only after the failure of each and every establishment strategy has been fully demonstrated to the potential mass base of such a revolution. And even beyond that fourth alternative comes the question of what such a revolution should try to accomplish, of its means and its ends.

Because it is my belief that the three visible roads will each prove to be incapable of solving certain basic American problems, involving particularly the relations among the races, my thesis is that a revolutionary situation potentially exists in this country. To say that it is not present now is irrelevant, for it is being prepared by the system and prepared for consciously by some elements in the population. What is relevant is to examine, sociologically and historically, the processes of revolution in an urban society, including its prerequisites, its organizational forms, its problems and tactics, and its possible outcomes.

In particular, I think it is important to examine the problems of revolution in a *premature* situation, one which is pre- or proto-revolutionary, rather than revolutionary in a real sense. First, what makes a situation premature, and what makes it "ripe"? Second, can a fully developed revolutionary situation be "helped along" by insurrectionary activity in a premature period? Third, what problems does pre-revolutionary activity create for the long-range revolution?

I will not attempt any new or grandiose theories of revolution, of insurrections, or of social movements. In general this will be a synthesis, derived largely from the work of other social scientists and those experienced in the practice of revolution. It will be a study mainly in the sense that the area to be covered has not been analyzed as a single body of material. The major focus will be on insurrection in the urban area.

I will proceed from the general to the specific: to know about urban insurrection it is necessary to know about revolution, which is one type of social movement, which in turn is a category within the general sociological field of collective behavior. Hence I begin with a discussion of the last mentioned, then narrow down to social movements, then to revolution, of which paramilitary, irregular, or "internal" war is only one species; a discussion of the urban insurrection (violent variety) begins in Chapter 4, and one alternative to it, nonviolent revolution (sometimes nowadays termed civilian defense), is discussed in Chapter 6.

Glancing quickly over the literature in this subject (and proceeding from the general to the more specific), there have been many books on the topics of revolution and social movements.[1] Yet, with the exception of basically historical works, such as those of Marx, Georges Lefebvre, or C. L. R. James,[2] not much has been written on specific revolutions by sociologists. And while sociologists have studied many specific movements, they have not examined violent ones that take the form of insurrection.

Again, within the field of sociology the work of such pioneers as Gustave LeBon [3] on crowds and mobs is well-known, but when riots become rebellions the sociologists seem often to leave the field to political scientists, who are frequently technicians when they are not military men outright. In the same way, warfare and violence in general, as types of conflict behavior, have been discussed by sociologists and political philosophers (for example, Raymond Aron, Hannah Arendt, or, at another level, Lewis Coser [4]), but when it comes to the specifics of, let us say, guerrilla warfare, we have little more than political treatises (Che Guevara, Regis Debray [5]) or technical manuals written for the armed forces (T. N. Greene [6]). Furthermore, these writings are limited entirely to the rural situation.

As far as the specific topic of this book is concerned—

again, with the exception of journalistic or personal memoirs, and a handful of references in a very few books (Feliks Gross [7] is an exception)—there are either technical "how-to-keep-them-down manuals such as Rex Applegate's,[8] or very limited "how-to-do-them" books on demonstrations (Oppenheimer and George Lakey [9]). Or one must be satisfied with journalistic endeavors of a technical bent oriented to taking advantage of the sensationalism of recent ghetto riots—for example, various efforts in *Ramparts* or *Esquire* [10] will have to do. This book will consequently try to skirt the twin dangers of over-general theorizing which has little applicability to the urban insurrection, and over-concern with the techniques of street fighting.

We must first attempt, briefly, some common understanding of terminology, or definitions. In particular, there has been a lot of trouble with the terms "revolution" and "rebellion." Chalmers Johnson [11] uses the term "rebellion" to mean the restoration of a previous, better society, so that it is often actually conservative from a historical standpoint. He reserves the term "revolution" to mean a fundamental alteration of social relationships toward something qualitatively new, not seen before.

This is akin to the anthropologist's distinction between a revitalization movement of the *revivalistic* kind, as opposed to one of the innovative sort.[12] A revitalization movement for the anthropologist is any ". . . deliberate, organized, conscious effort by members of a society to construct a more satisfying culture," [13] so that it can be oriented toward a previous state of society or toward a view of some more ideal future situation; the former would be considered a revivalistic movement, the latter an innovative one. For example, Goldwaterism or Birchism might be considered revivalistic; communism and socialism are innovative (with respect to the United States at any rate), while both elements are present within the broad spectrum of Black Protest—the Muslims and

other Africa-oriented movements are at least somewhat revivalistic, while all black movements are also innovative in
the sense that a new and better society (never before seen on
these shores) is desired.

While I think Chalmers Johnson has confused us with his
usage of the term rebellion, I shall follow his definition of
revolution to mean "a sweeping, fundamental change in
political organization, social structure, economic property
control, and the predominant myth of social order, thus indi-
cating a major break in the continuity of development." [14]

This kind of revolution is of course distinct from "the industrial revolution," or "the population explosion." These are,
it is true, also revolutions; they entail sweeping changes and
major breaks in the continuity of development. That is, at
some point a quantitative change becomes a qualitative one.
But that break generally is not a *purposive* or planned one,
although specific incidents such as family planning may be;
and while it may be possible in *retrospect* to identify the
point of the qualitative change, or break, it can rarely be
done at the time. A revolution, as the term is used here,
involves a *sudden* turnover or alteration, taking from as
short a time as a few hours to, perhaps, the course of a civil
war. Further, it almost inevitably involves a change in the
control of *social power* (by which is meant more than a
simple shift in office-holding personnel, involving at least some
fundamental economic change) from one *group* to another,
these groups representing in themselves the quality of other
changes taking place. For example, that group which took
power in Petrograd in November 1917 consisted of a different *class* of person than the group it replaced. The revolution
did not simply result in shuffling personnel within the same
kind of group.

A revolutionary outbreak that has not yet succeeded can
be called a rebellion, an uprising or rising, or an insurrection;
or if the intended change is relatively minor (for example,

only a change in personnel rather than a change in the kind of group), then it can be called a *coup* or a *putsch,* although these also imply a more limited number of participants—they are basically elitist affairs. It is true that elitist coups can *lead* to revolution in the true sense, but in such cases it is not the actual coup that is revolutionary; rather, the revolution stems from decisions taken by the new power group *after* the old order has been overthrown. On the other hand, it is rarely the case that a *successful* mass rebellion is anything short of revolutionary in its outcome. For various reasons, it is driven to be revolutionary even if this was not at first intended.

A "social movement" is more encompassing as a term. All revolutions, uprisings, rebellions, and insurrections reflect social movements; coups sometimes do, but less directly (for example, the "Decembrists" in Russia in 1825 [15]). But of course social movements take many other forms as well. For the time being, two definitions will suffice: a movement is ". . . pluralistic behavior functioning as an organized mass effort directed toward a change of established folkways or institutions." [16] Note that while it always involves large numbers, it does not necessarily require a *break* in the continuity of development, as when a child is born, or when boiling water turns to steam, both revolutionary developments. A second definition of social movement might be that of the revitalization movement cited earlier.

Finally, the terms guerrilla, partisan, irregular, and insurgent must be defined. I shall subsume all of these (reserving thoroughgoing discussion for a later chapter) under the term "paramilitary warfare," which I take to mean any behavior (usually, but not always violent, as we shall also see later) of an organized sort directed either defensively or offensively against the military forces (including police) of the dominant power in society, by military elements associated with no regular or recognized government (though it may be in exile). It implies some minimal political goal (as distinct from banditry or gangsterism) and may include a range of activities such as terrorism, an underground movement, a putschist conspiracy, or an actual outbreak of rebellion at some point which seeks as its goal the seizure of the government or the overturn of the social order.

"Social science in general," writes Harry Eckstein,[17] "has been too much concerned with fashioning tools . . . too little with the direct processing of concrete experience . . ." This is particularly true of the fields of collective behavior, social movements, revolution, and insurrection. In terms of rigorous social scientific method, such phenomena are not easy to study; surveys cannot often be administered, such events cannot be observed through one-way mirrors, nor can controlled experiments be set up. Consequently, academics are reluctant to stake their reputations on thin evidence lest they be proven wrong. Yet rigorous methodology all too often limits one to working on the insignificant; the social scientist must choose, sometimes, to accept higher risks of being wrong in order to work in important fields.

Today nothing can be more important than revolution; my own view coincides with that of Lenin, who wrote that "it is more pleasant and useful to go through the 'experience of the revolution' than to write about it." But it may be that my generation was born "too late for the War, too soon for the Revolution," so let us at least see what can be learned from the past and present so that whatever happens, the tragedies of history can be minimized.

CHAPTER ONE

COLLECTIVE BEHAVIOR

The study of collective behavior embraces everything from disasters (as the result of such natural events as volcanic eruptions or hurricanes, or as the result of accidents or war, such as industrial explosions or thermonuclear attacks) and "extreme situations" (such as those confronting inmates of concentration or extermination camps) to expressive behavior such as panty raids, religious cults and drugs, riots, and crowd behavior, and the study of masses, publics, social movements, and revolution. All collective behavior involves the less stable, less predictable, less formal aspects of group life. Its situations are those in which the usual norms of behavior have been disrupted, causing the development of new norms and new values.[1]

Collective behavior, however, represents only one end of a range of sociological investigation. The other end is that field of study usually termed complex, or formal, organizations, the study of bureaucracies. In a sense, we begin with informal, unstable, behavior and culminate with formal, structured, stable, predictable behavior. But this does not mean an "either-or" situation, for even in the most informal kinds of behavior we can often see the beginnings of formal structure, the beginnings of organization; conversely, even within (perhaps especially within) the most rigid bureaucracies we can also see all sorts of informal, spontaneous behavior.

Social movements, as many observers have recognized, have a tendency to begin with informality, spontaneity, and face-to-face relationships. Gradually they become more formal, more structured, developing bureaucratic routines and relationships in which individuals are treated more bureaucratically. This process, sometimes called "the routinization of charisma" (after Max Weber, one of the first to discuss it in any conceptual detail), has often been interpreted in a pessimistic way; it has been seen as some kind of "iron law of oligarchy" which undermines even the best and most idealistically motivated efforts of mankind.

Along this continuum between collective behavior and behavior in the setting of complex organizations, the phenomena of social movements, revolutions, and insurrections assume an intermediary place. While movements which culminate in insurrection often begin on a very informal level, as they begin to formulate specific political goals (including, perhaps, the overthrow of government) they are forced to develop organizational structures to accomplish those goals. Even in the situation of a most spontaneous outbreak—for example, an urban riot—the rioters must then or later develop a more formal organization if their objectives are to have any longer-range meaning. Even within a riot, as it takes place, organization develops: tasks are allocated, a division of labor develops, guards are posted, certain groups have the job of tearing down the metal lattices which protect store windows, and the like. And the riot itself can be seen as an early, perhaps "primitive" form of political organization, a form of organization which I shall call "proto-political," in the sense that more specifically ideological politics usually follow, at least in the Western urban setting.

COLLECTIVE BEHAVIOR AND CHANGE

All collective behavior is related to some sort of social change. Even a natural disaster is a change from the normal, though only on a local level; hence reactions to such change tend not to take a political form. On the other hand, a nationwide revolution is a reaction to a series of changes on a macro-level. In turn, collective behavior creates other changes, so that the student of such phenomena always has a difficult time separating the symptom from the causes. For example: one response of young people to what has been called "alienation" is the use of drugs. This contributes to the creation of an expressive movement (the "hippies") which calls forth repressive measures by the police. The repression in turn creates further alienation. It then becomes difficult to distinguish causes: Do police cause alienation? Does the use of drugs cause repression? In other words, the existence of a movement, regardless of cause, changes the situation so that whatever happens must be in response to the new, not to the old, pre-movement situation if it is to make sense. But most observers agree that the normal or stable social order (even while constantly, almost imperceptibly, undergoing some change) must be significantly disrupted before masses of people engage in collective behavior, particularly in a social movement.

A common term used to signify this disruption, particularly as it affects individuals, is that of "strain." That is, society is in one sense a system of many elements that are linked in complex patterns. Each element in a system is also a kind of "sub-system," consisting in turn of other elements. Alterations in these elements, and in the links among them and between them and their sub-systems or larger systems (super-systems or meta-systems), all cause structural strain. Other elements must "catch up" or change in turn so as to remove strain and enable the system to function once more in more normal terms. Since change is inevitable, structural strains are constantly present in social systems; and when there are deeply serious strains, or multiples of them, in a social system, it can no longer cope with its problems. In such circumstances the strains in the system affect many individuals so that they organize themselves to make the kinds of changes in the system they see as necessary to the creation of "a more satisfying culture." They seek a system in which strains have been alleviated sufficiently as far as the participants are concerned.

The sources of these strains, or "dysfunctions," in a system can be many. Anthropologists emphasize the role of invention, or the introduction of new technologies as the result of contacts between a receiving culture and a "donor" culture. Sociologists often emphasize the role of deviant individuals and idiosyncratic behavior; historical sociologists also talk about the strain inherent in the development of successive stages of society. The term "culture lag" has become famous as one way of interpreting social strains stemming from the fact that technology often changes faster, within a system, than the "super-structural" institutions of that society, such as law, family system, education, and so forth, so that these institutions are no longer appropriate to the new technology. This means that a strain between the technology (or economy) of a society and its superstructure (its other institutions) develops, and this strain creates many problems for many individuals, hence for society as a whole. To some degree this is also the Marxian view. The solution to such a problem is to bring the institutions of society into line with the more advanced technology —but because the institutions are run by power structures which resist being displaced and changed, such change often implies revolution. A current example might be the effects of automation or cybernation on other institutions of society, for example, the value system which states that "he who does not work, neither shall he eat." A revolution at least in that particular value seems to be prerequisite to solving the strain between that value and the technological reality that many people soon will be permanently unemployable and technologically unnecessary.

Strain, then, implies an ambiguous situation. As the above example suggests, ambiguities concerning a value are only one kind of strain. The old answers of society no longer work, at least for some people; hence unpredictability results, and the individual is confronted with conflicting interpretations of events. These conflicts create for him a "consciousness of maladjustment [which] creates an internal tension which leads the maladjusted individual to consider his situation." [2] As Anthony Wallace puts it:

> . . . the system . . . is unable to make possible the reliable satisfaction of certain values which are held to be essential . . . The mazeway of a culturally disillusioned person, accordingly, is an image of a world that is unpredictable, or barren in its simplicity, or both. His mood . . . will be one of panic-stricken anxiety, shame, guilt, depression, or apathy.[3]

The strain in society often leads to "large numbers of people . . . seeking answers they do not have, reassurances that the answers they do have are right, or ways of implementing answers . . . ," [4] hence we see "an atmosphere conducive to even the most bizarre proposals, many of which thrive and grow. Providing answers and offering durable ideals are part of the 'promise' of many movements."

The particular shape and form of a movement (for example, whether it is reformist in nature, or revolutionary; whether it takes the form of Melanesian cargo cults or modern trade unionism or civil rights sit-ins) depends first of all on the historical context of the situation—we would hardly expect Detroit automobile workers to develop cargo cults. Second, it depends on the particular kind or kinds of strain in the situation; and finally, there are such tactical considerations as leadership, perception of degree of opposition, perception of the likelihood of society fulfilling promises, and the like.

KINDS OF STRAIN

What kinds of strain are there, aside from ambiguities among values (for example, "Thou shalt not kill" versus "Thou shalt report for induction"), or between values and conditions (for example, the value of work versus the condition of unemployability)? Several are of particular importance to students of revolution. One concerns ambiguity in the allocation of resources to various sectors of society, that is, what groups get how much of the political, economic, and prestige resources available. This ambiguity has to do with the stratification or class structure of the society. Of course, most societies usually are not ambiguous about this; there is no strain until some large number of individuals see themselves as deprived. Almost always they are those in the subordinate strata, that is, the poor, the oppressed, the "disadvantaged," workers, farmers, or, as seen from "the top," "the dangerous classes" who, in this kind of strain, have an interest in change. As Allan Silver points out, the literature of police work abounds with perennial themes of potential disorder in the urban setting which call for military steps to contain these dangerous classes. The social order is again and again threatened by, variously, the poor, workers, sailors, immigrants, criminals, the lumpenproletariat, and various combinations of them, and the police have historically had as their mission the control of these elements on behalf of the propertied.[5]

The term "deprivation" is commonly used to describe ambiguity in the allocation of economic resources, but resources of power and prestige can also be involved. Moreover, it is rarely deprivation as such which accounts for strain. Rather, the deprivation must first be *perceived* by a group, and this can only be done if the group can compare itself with some other relevant group. The group must see itself deprived *relative* to some other group; hence the concept "relative deprivation." This other group may be beneath it, above it, similar to it but in another country, or even itself at an earlier time. And the deprivation may be perceived because the group has become more miserable while its reference group is becoming miserable at a lesser rate; or it is becoming miserable while its reference group is stationary; or it is stationary while its reference group is improving; or it is actually improving, but its reference group is improving faster, as is the case for black Americans in terms of absolute income.

There are strains other than deprivation, and while they are important in creating conditions leading to social movements, they are probably not quite as important as deprivation in leading to revolutionary activity. To mention some of them briefly: there is the ambiguity in society as to how resources will be allocated to fulfill different social tasks (for example, the war on poverty versus the war in Vietnam); there is ambiguity in an organization as to how to keep itself going (shall students be allowed to participate more, or shall they be deprived of participation in order to keep an educational bureaucracy going?); there is the ambiguity stemming from the difference between how one performs and how one is rewarded (do we get what we think we are worth, relative to others like us?); there is the ambiguity stemming from conflict among our many statuses and roles in society (father-employee; emancipated woman–housewife; maturing adult–sheltered student; teacher–researcher; black American–middle-class American; and so on); there is the ambiguity of the means by which different sectors of society compete for resources, that is, what is sanctioned by the social and legal structure (if it is all right for the police to murder members of the Black Panther party, why is it not all right for the Panthers to go about armed? If it is all right for university bureaucrats to refuse significant communication by giving people the old bureaucratic run-around, why is it not all right for students to communicate with their bodies by preventing the machinery from functioning until communication takes place?).

Finally, and perhaps inevitably, there is the ambiguity described by Freud: the conflict between individual self-expression and the group's need to survive, that is, the struggle between self and society, id and superego.

Perhaps it should be emphasized that no movement, no revolution deals with only one strain, one ambiguity; particularly in the *form* in which people try to cope with the disintegration of their "mazeways," we see the interplay of many kinds of strains. The form of collective behavior is determined by many things. So many things seem to determine the existence of a movement at a specific time that such determinants are sometimes far more than are "needed"; hence we say that the situation is "overdetermined." For example, it would seem that "sexual inhibition alters the structure of the economically suppressed individual in such a manner that he thinks, feels, and acts against his own material interests," according to Wilhelm Reich.[6] We cannot, at present, prove Reich's particular point, but it illustrates how for some theorists at least even the unconscious can alter the political nature of a movement. As Reich puts it, "The practical problem of mass psychology, then, is that of activating the passive majority of the population . . . end the elimination of the inhibitions which counteract the will to freedom . . . If the psychic energies of the average mass of people watching a football game . . . could be diverted into the rational channels of a freedom movement, they would be invincible."

Revolutionary movements, while also overdetermined, are largely related to that strain stemming from perceived deprivation of society's resources in economic goods and services, political power, or social prestige. Within the field of sociology, the study of such movements has to do with the study of large (secondary) groups along a continuum from informal collective behavior to formal complex-organizational behavior. Now let us look more specifically at paramilitary activities from the sociological viewpoint.[7]

I have already implied that rebellion is one kind of social movement among many, involving a collective effort to create a more satisfying culture or to protect some aspect of the culture against a perceived threat to it. Strain of one kind or another is what motivates individuals to participate in movements; thus the prerequisite to insurrection, too, is that the status quo is seen as inadequate to the solution of certain problems as they are felt by some group in the population. In addition, the group must be desperate enough to feel that only a military strategy can bring about, or prevent, the desired, or undesired, change. The tactical issue then often becomes whether the group is capable of accomplishing its goal, especially in the face of the armed opposition of the "establishment."

Armed insurrection can obviously be distinguished from other kinds of collective behavior because it involves violence directed toward the immediate or ultimate overthrow of the established order, or, in the case of defensive insurrections, toward the defense of a sub-group of society against the further encroachments of the established order—two rather different types. But once violence and a posture vis-à-vis the status quo have been established, the picture takes on several other dimensions.

INSURRECTION AS COLLECTIVE BEHAVIOR

One set of variables which may help to clarify the picture and put insurrection into a perspective is that of (a) involvement or interaction and (b) formal organization.

We begin with apathy, disillusionment, or depression. As apathy is dispelled by a particular situation—for example, the development of a movement or the appearance of a charismatic leader—the individual becomes more involved as he seeks to "resynthesize" his way of life, values, behaviors so as to make more sense out of his situation. But there are degrees of involvement—some interaction may be with movements which in fact reject interaction as their goal, or perhaps as their tactic. For example, religious separatism, the escapism of utopian communities, or some aspects of the drug culture do not seek interaction. Tactically, involvement may be in a movement which advocates a strike or boycott, which is a withdrawal from interaction with an opponent (though not from society). Interaction with an opponent (say, the police, or "the power structure") increases in other kinds of demonstrations such as picket lines, and is brought to an extreme in the tactics of direct action (sit-ins, seizures of plants or buildings, marches on public offices, and so forth). In the same way, interaction with an opponent or at least with his symbolic representations (his property) increases in a riot, but decreases if a mob is dispersed by the authorities. Mobs can therefore move in a focal way, toward an objective, in which case they increase interaction; or they can flee and disperse, in which case interaction is decreased.

But mobs differ from demonstrations in that they are less structured, less organized—hence the dimension of organization. And they differ from inactivity or dispersal—hence the dimension of interaction. Therefore, when we have no organization and no interaction we have apathy or flight; when we have organization but no interaction we have utopian withdrawal, a boycott, or a strike; when we have interaction but no organization we have a mob or a riot; when we have both organization and interaction we have political demonstrations, revolutionary activity, and, sometimes, insurrectionary warfare.

One key to paramilitary or guerrilla warfare is that interaction is sporadic. It includes hit-and-run tactics and withdrawal in the face of superior force. Only at the actual point of seizure of the government (or its attempt), that is, a general outbreak of revolutionary activity possibly as the closing stage of an extended guerrilla war, do we see full interaction with the opponent—unless the opponent chooses to flee at that point, as was the case of Batista in Cuba.

A distinction from nonviolent protest activity needs to be made here as well. Obviously, paramilitary activity involves violence; but it is often combined with various other forms of direct action, some of which, like strikes, can be and often are conducted on a nonviolent or at least on an a-violent basis. Thus civil disobedience sometimes operates in tandem with criminal disobedience (rebellion), although if a paramilitary force is actually operating, all disobedience will be perceived by the authorities as criminal and in the same category with the rebellion, and will be similarly punished. This is an important point, for it largely rebuts recent arguments which say that a little disruption, rioting, and violence does not harm "the movement," and that the movement therefore need not openly disavow violence and explicitly espouse nonviolence. For if a movement is not explicitly nonviolent, it will be treated as if it were its most violent part. Even if a movement is nonviolent it may be perceived and treated as if it were violent. This strategic point will reappear later.

TYPES OF VIOLENT PROTEST

Three dimensions of violent protest are of particular interest: (1) a historical dimension involving the rural-urban continuum; (2) an associated dimension involving degree of political consciousness; and (3) an independent dimension related to the distinction between a coup or putsch and a revolution, that of numbers of people involved. By rural-urban continuum I mean basically the issue of whether the countryside or the city is to be the focus of insurrectionary activity. By political consciousness I mean whether a particular insurrectionary or violent effort has some kind of political ideology, or whether it is basically a pre-political or proto-political endeavor. By the distinction between coup and revolution, and numbers of people involved, I mean generally whether the contemplated social change is to be undertaken by a relatively small number of men, an elite, from the top down, or whether the change is to involve a real movement, masses of people, with the strategy of change being from the bottom up. The latter would include movements led by elites but involving masses of people as the instruments of change in some major way.

There are, as I see it, eight variations on these three dimensions, four in a rural context and four in an urban setting, as shown in outline form on the following page. (Note that a check mark indicates whether the setting is rural or urban, a plus or a minus indicates the presence or absence of political consciousness and mass participation.)

There are four variations within each setting; these show a historical development, that is, the normal historical progression is from the first variation through the second and third type, to the fourth. The first two variations, then, are pre-political or proto-political movements; the second two are more modern, politically oriented revolutionary movements.

	RURAL/URBAN	POLITICAL CONSCIOUSNESS	MASS PARTICIPATION
social banditry, vendettas, early Mafia	√	−	−
peasant uprisings, revitalization movements	√	−	+
guerrilla bands	√	+	−
guerrilla liberation army (Zapata, FLN, NFL, etc.)	√	+	+
gangsterism, contemporary Mafia, jacket clubs, hooliganism	√	−	−
riots, vandalism, looting	√	−	+
terrorism (selective assassination, possibly leading to a coup)	√	+	−
rebellion or "rising"	√	+	+

Note, too, that each type of movement has an analogy in the other setting, as follows:

RURAL		URBAN
social banditry	=	gangsterism
peasant uprisings	=	riots
guerrilla bands	=	terrorism
liberation army	=	rebellion or "rising"

In order properly to understand urban paramilitary activity, each of these eight variations or ideal types must be seen in historical context.

The social bandit has perhaps been best described by E. J. Hobsbawm: "A man becomes a bandit because he does something which is not regarded as criminal by his local conven-

tions, but is so regarded by the State or the local rulers." [8]
He is a Robin Hood, a Pretty Boy Floyd, a Jesse James, or
at least he is so regarded by the local population from which
he comes. The social bandit existed as a type in southern Italy
as recently as the 1940's; the rise to dominance of an urban-
industrial culture usually marks the end of the rural bandit.
Bands of such people are usually small, no larger than thirty,
and their victims tend to be members or representatives of
the upper strata in the society: rich merchants, clergy, lawyers,
politicians. Bandits were often successful, being protected by
the people of their area; they seldom strayed outside. Occasionally they became prosperous, poor boys who "made good,"
thus making banditry one road to upper mobility in situations
where most other roads were closed to the common man.
(There are certain parallels here with James Hoffa, or Adam
Clayton Powell, in the urban setting; but they should not be
overdrawn, obviously.) A bandit's standard ending was that
of death by betrayal, or, on the other hand, to become a thug
for the upper class—which is pretty much what happened to
a lot of *mafiosi* in Sicily. The bandit, then, is rural and pre-
political; his strength is inverse to organized, political agrarian
movements, but like such movements it grows with hard times
—precisely when the bandit, due to his lack of ideology, is
least able to have solutions. The bandit can therefore set
limits to oppression (by terrorizing the oppressor), but he
cannot really solve it. People with guns but without ideology
are bandits; people with ideology but without guns are liberals,
and in a rural setting in which the oppressor classes rule with
violence, they are impotent.

The analogous social formation in the urban area is the
gangster, or, on a less organized level, the juvenile fighting
gang. The gangster-racketeer represents an outgrowth of the
Mafia, or rather, a more formalized, better-organized and
urbanized version of it, but often historically related to the
rural and small town Mafia of Sicily.[9] Like the rural bandit,

his career begins, often enough, by violating laws not re-garded by his neighborhood culture as real violations. He is stigmatized by a criminal record, and legitimate roads to up-ward mobility are subsequently closed to him. Like the rural bandit, he basically accepts society's system of goals (material rewards), but he must innovate illicit means to attain those goals. He is seldom as "social" (helpful to his people) as the rural bandit, but from time to time urban gangs (mainly ju-veniles, not racketeers) go "social," that is, abandon fighting and adopt tasks of a "social welfare" character, such as recreation, clean-up campaigns, and so forth.

PEASANT WARS AND URBAN RIOTS

Peasant uprisings (chiefly European) and revitalization move-ments, their equivalent in the colonial or underdeveloped nation, have been amply described in sociological, anthropo-logical, and historical literature.[10] Semi- or pre-feudal slave uprisings (Nat Turner, for example) would be included in this category. The basic distinction between a peasant uprising and rural banditry is that the uprising is generally of shorter duration (although a series of uprisings can follow one upon another so as to make for virtually a half-century of warfare, as in central Europe from about 1478 to about 1527), has somewhat more specific goals (usually of a revivalistic or historically reactionary sort, that is, oriented toward the restoration of some previous, ostensibly better, condition), and involves significant masses of people on a more or less spontaneous, relatively unorganized basis. The level of politi-cal consciousness, given populations that are at best semi-literate, is still fairly low, though individual peasant leaders (Emiliano Zapata in Mexico) or leaders of the peasants (Thomas Münzer, 1498–1525, a theologian) may have more developed ideas.

Incidents having the characteristics of a peasant war took

place in the United States as recently as the 1930's. Widespread suffering, especially by day laborers and sharecroppers in the South following a decline in cotton prices, led to a series of strikes, attempted seizures of homes and work implements by sheriffs, and harassment and persecution of union organizers. In response, proto-revolutionary outbreaks, including armed resistance to sheriffs and their deputies, took place on a wide scale. In one incident, armed blacks barricaded a house when police came to seize the property, and in the ensuing gunfight the sheriff and two deputies were wounded and one black killed.[11]

The urban analogy to the peasant uprising, again politically one step advanced from gangsterism, though still a proto-political kind of activity, is the riot. Before full participation in parliamentary democracy in England, the streets had been a more or less legitimate arena in which to make demands on elites; it was a "proto-democratic system." In the eighteenth and nineteenth centuries, the streets were used so that "the unorganized poor . . . might articulately address the propertied classes through riot and disorder."[12] Current debates as to whether ghetto riots are class- or race-based, or whether they are "merely" criminal or more in the nature of rebellions, are a clue to seeing the riot as a "proto-political" development. "The riot," as Tom Hayden says, "is certainly an awkward, even primitive form of history-making. But if people are barred from using the sophisticated instruments of the established order for their ends, they will find another way."[13] There would not be much point here in analyzing urban riots in more detail; the literature has been voluminous in the last few years.[14] It is enough to say that there is now general agreement on underlying causes and immediate precipitants. Stanley Lieberson and Arnold Silverman "see the riot in terms of institutional malfunctioning or a racial difficulty which is not met—and perhaps cannot be met—by existing social institutions." Anthony Oberschall talks about "the situation of the lower-class urban Negroes outside of the South," and the fact that the civil rights gains of the past years "have not removed the fundamental sources of grievances of a large proportion of the Negro population in the U.S." The "Riot Commission" notes that "Segregation and poverty have created in the racial ghetto a destructive environment totally unknown to most white Americans . . . white society is deeply implicated in the ghetto. White institutions created it, white institutions maintain it, and white society condones it." Riots have provided more than ample data supporting the basic premise discussed earlier, that of "structural strain," as being the single best overall (though perhaps over-general) framework within which to discuss all collective behavior.

What is particularly interesting, however, is that the urban riot (and, by implication, the peasant uprising), is seen by a number of observers as a step in the direction of a more politically conscious movement. Historically, it would seem, urban mobs and riots give way to more sophisticated political forms, such as modern social movements (trade unionism, for example, or working-class political parties), where such forms are feasible. In an authoritarian society (czarism, for example) where reforms are not sufficiently forthcoming, or where democratic outlets are excluded, riots are replaced by revolutionary movements involving armed insurrection.

Hayden puts it this way: "Men are now appearing in the ghettos who might turn the energy of the riot in a more organized and continuous revolutionary direction . . . During a riot, for instance, a conscious guerrilla can participate in pulling police away from the path of people engaged in attacking stores . . ." [15] And it is only a step from this riot with auxiliary guerrillas to the urban insurrection as such. The transition in the individual's consciousness between urban rioting and insurrection, including guerrilla warfare, is no longer difficult to make. In fact, as Harold Black and Marvin Labes point out, the analogy has been made for some time by police.[16] Ghetto areas are considered enemy territory; the police are "at war" with criminal elements; it becomes less and less possible to differentiate between ordinary citizens and criminals (just as in guerrilla warfare); the innocent thereupon begin to suffer harassment and to identify with "criminal elements," and see the police as a common enemy. Constitutional rights (a domestic equivalent of the Geneva Convention) become hindrances to the police in their "war." Subsequently, better "community relations" are called for—imaginative "social programs" must be developed by the police. But, as in Vietnam or elsewhere, the police are alienated from the population by the fact that these social programs are in tandem with policies of massive repression; so the police, like the Green Berets, are seen as hypocritical, and the social programs as merely a subterfuge. The "two-war" strategy fails, both in the ghetto and in the countryside, as a strategy with which to divide the civilian population from "criminal elements" or guerrillas. (And, under this kind of strategy, the line between the criminal or bandit and the guerrilla begins to disappear; the bandit and the criminal become more political, hence revolutionary.)

The population, too, begins to see this parallel. Irving Louis Horowitz and Martin Liebowitz talk about the "Latinization of Negro riot and student revolts," by which they mean the "breakdown in the distinction between crime and marginal politics." The Blackstone Rangers, a Chicago juvenile gang, now engage in various kinds of political activities (as an alternative, however, to military solutions). But Horowitz and Liebowitz point out that "In the absence of acceptable political solutions, it is probable that increasing reliance upon domestic military solutions will be sought."

Similarly, the proto-political formation of the countryside, social banditry, in turn tends to be replaced by modern guerrilla warfare. In the developing nations, the parallel is that of the revitalization movement, which often develops into the modern national independence movement. Members of the subordinate culture suffering various kinds of strain move away; they go abroad to a university; they are conscripted into the police or constabulary, or into the armed forces; they go to work in the home country of a colonial power. Everywhere they come into contact with new ideas, frequently revolutionary ideas. They return home to infuse a proto-political, proto-national, proto-revolutionary movement with modern political, nationalist, revolutionary ideas. Today's college student, visiting from abroad, is tomorrow's political prisoner, and the day after tomorrow is the prime minister—to capsulize a part of the career of Kwame Nkrumah.

The four categories discussed in this chapter, and the final four to be discussed in the next, constitute "ideal types," and as such they rarely exist in pure form. For example, an urban rebellion is almost invariably accompanied by individualistic, non-political (or pre-political) acts of a gangsterish sort, such as hooliganism, and is frequently also accompanied by what can be called proto-political behavior, such as rioting, looting, or even ethnic pogroms. (Looting of Jewish-owned stores in black ghetto areas, while not a pogrom in the classical sense, does border on that. On the other hand, looting by police or army units of black-owned stores is a nearly perfect example of the classical pogrom, but this is not done as part of an insurrection by the oppressed group; on the contrary, it is done to keep the oppressed group in line, which, again, is what the classical pogrom under czarism in part was intended to do.)

Individualistic political acts such as terrorism are often integrated into what are destined to become mass revolutionary movements. An intermediate phenomenon, the "resistance movement," or underground, typical of the occupied nations of World War II, also involves individualistic acts carefully integrated into a master plan ultimately involving masses of people.

The purpose of this chapter has been to put insurrectionary warfare into the context of social movements and collective behavior theory, particularly in terms of underlying social causes and structure or organization. Next I shall discuss the last two steps in the historical development from social banditry to revolution, namely guerrilla bands in the countryside and their analogy, the terrorist group in the city; and finally a national liberation army in the countryside, and its analogy, the urban insurrection.

CHAPTER TWO

THE COUNTRYSIDE VERSUS THE CITY

The final four types of violent protest—guerrilla bands and the liberation army (both rural-based), and terrorism and rebellion (both urban)—can be discussed more fruitfully by distinguishing certain basic issues that divide them than by briefly describing each. The two urban types, in any case, will be described in detail in Chapter 4.

The basic division among these types reflects a division among all revolutionists of the left in the twentieth century: is the lever for social change to be the peasantry or the urban working class; and shall the revolution be "from above" or "from below," that is, elitist-oriented or oriented toward mass participation? Whether one talks of the guerrilla band (such as Fidel Castro's group in the early days in the Sierra Maestra, or Guevara's group in Bolivia) or urban terrorism (for example, armed attacks on police or occupying armed forces), these are the tactics of elitism; whether one talks of peasant armies (such as that of Emiliano Zapata) or of urban uprisings (the Paris Commune), both imply mass participation. At the same time, small band or big army, is it to come from the countryside to all of society, or from the city? Let us first consider the issue of a rural versus an urban context.

THE URBAN INTELLECTUAL TRADITION

Basically, the tradition of the Western Enlightenment is an urban tradition, one which has seen the urban area as a center of culture and a civilizing force. The countryside is crude and vulgar, the bastion of narrow-minded and reactionary traditions. It is not hard to see why this attitude should have been so. It was, after all, an outgrowth of the struggle of the modern bourgeoisie against feudalism, a struggle which so often in history—even now in the Third World—pits the urban centers against tribalism and village life.

Marxism always looked to the urban working class as the vehicle for historic change; yet today it is either the urban lumpenproletarian, the unemployed and semi-criminal element (in Marx's terms), or the peasant who forms the ranks of revolutionaries—though, as always, the leaders are mainly the alienated sons and daughters of the middle and upper classes. Marx and his followers, as they readily confessed, came out of the bourgeois Enlightenment tradition. They were city people, and their analysis of history saw the city as the key, and the city's vast population of working-class people as the hope, for change. The peasantry was a dependent force, leaning upon some other social class for its historical role. "They were scattered over large areas," writes Engels in his *Peasant War in Germany,* "and this made every agreement between them extremely difficult; the old habit of submission inherited generation from generation . . . all combined to keep the peasant quiet." And Marx, in his *18th Brumaire,* pointing to the phenomenon of Bonapartism and how peasants fall into the habit of supporting Bonapartes, talks of how "The small-holding peasants form a vast mass, the members of which live in similar conditions, but without entering into manifold relations with one another . . . the identity of their interests begets no community, no national bond . . . they are consequently incapable of enforcing their class interest in their own name . . . they cannot represent themselves, they must be represented." And so they are, by dictators in general—Hitler's supporters came disproportionately from among the small farmers, too. In *The British Rule in India,* Marx shows his urban predilections even more as he describes India's "idyllic village communities" functioning to "restrain the human mind within the smallest possible compass, making it the unresisting tool of superstition, enslaving it beneath traditional rules, . . . [an] undignified, stagnatory, and vegetative life . . ."

In different ways and with different emphases, all of the well-known Marxist writers shared this basic view, including Lenin, Trotsky, and Rosa Luxemburg. Trotsky perhaps went furthest in terms of the peasantry's capacity to rule society: "Historical experience," Trotsky wrote, "shows that the peasantry [is] absolutely incapable of taking up an *independent* political role." Why? Because the peasants are ". . . unorganized, scattered, isolated from the towns, the nerve centers of politics and culture; stupid, limited in their horizons to the confines of their respective villages, indifferent to everything the town was thinking . . ."; thus the classical view of the urban intellectual. In the final analysis, ". . . the peasantry, because of its intermediate position and the heterogeneity of its social composition, . . . is compelled," said Trotsky, "in the revolutionary epoch, to choose between the policy of the bourgeoisie and the policy of the proletariat." [1]

While I think Trotsky and the classical Marxists were and

are right about the peasant's dependent role, Trotsky, because he stuck so rigidly to a two-class analysis ("either the bourgeoisie or the proletariat") was very wrong when it came to where the peasants would line up or how they would function in future society. Even Marx had gone beyond Trotsky in emphasizing the peasants' support for the two Napoleons—Bonaparte and Louis. And this was a clue. For Trotsky failed to see what Milovan Djilas later called "The New Class" as a factor—that is, the gradual rise to power during the 1920's in the Soviet Union of a *third* group, the bureaucracy *as a class,* opposed to the workers *and* anti-capitalist. The phenomenon which we today know as Stalinism was something Trotsky never really understood. To summarize, the New Class analysis says that in the absence of a strong bourgeoisie, and in the absence of an active, participating, conscious working class, the revolution must fall into the hands of a bureacracy—and the peasants, in this vacuum, also support (or at least are incapable of combating) the bureaucracy, the new elite.

This is precisely what has happened in the developing nations since World War II. The communist revolutions, as I would interpret them, have been supported by the peasants and have really been made by the peasants, or at least have been defended by them after the revolution. Where Trotsky urged the working class to get support from the peasants by expropriating the landlords and the bourgeoisie, in the absence of an active working class the vanguard Communist party elite has done the same, and the peasants have supported it as they would have supported anyone who accomplished this goal. The peasant-supported communist and nationalist revolutions in the third world have had as their ultimate *class content* (to use a Marxian idea) the rise to power of a bureaucratic elite supported by the peasants. To put this into an even smaller nutshell, the rule is this: if there is no democratically oriented working-class revolutionary movement to carry out a historically inevitable revolution, it will be carried out anyhow—but the failure of the working class means the success of the vanguard party, the accession of the elite to power as the new ruling class. The peasants can make a revolution, but they cannot, by their nature, carry it through. This must be done in the cities, by the government. So it is done by the peasants' leaders—and these are seldom if ever peasants (Castro, and so forth); or if they are, they don't remain so.

A socialist observer, discussing the very pertinent Vietnam example, puts it this way: "First of all, it is necessary to keep clear in our minds the difference between the *mass base* of a party or movement, and its *class basis;* . . . the fact that the mass base of the NLF lies among the peasantry does not mean that the NLF is controlled by the peasantry, or that an NLF victory will establish peasant control of the state and its society. Instead, the NLF is controlled by an incipient bureaucratic ruling class—that is its class basis, and that is the class which would be projected into state power by an NLF victory." [2] The fact is that while there have been many peasant uprisings (especially if one includes in this term the revitalization and proto-nationalist movements of the developing nations), there has never been a successful one—if by successful is meant a seizure of power in society, and a holding on to it over a significant time. The closest to that came when Emiliano Zapata took Mexico City in 1914 in the civil war; but he went home to see to the crops and, as predicted, his enemies were not far behind.

PEASANT ROMANTICISM

The key to the romantic view of peasant life, on the other hand (as well as to the perspective which sees the peasant as a motor force in history), is that of the *Gemeinschaft* or integrated community which the peasant village is supposed to represent. It is contrasted to the segmented, atomized urban *Gesellschaft* or society. The peasant community implies a community of fate, an attachment to family and village, an ethos which reveres agricultural work and is hostile to town ways, commerce, and the corruption that allegedly accompanies urbanization. While the peasant may be a helpless victim of environment, he is not alienated in the modern sense; *Gemeinschaft* suggests that people are treated as total persons, that is, in sociologist Talcott Parsons' terms, as "role-diffuse," while the urbanite is treated separately from one role to another, or in terms of "role specificity." "Specificity-diffuseness," says Seymour Martin Lipset, "refers to the difference between treating individuals in terms of the specific positions which they happen to occupy, rather than diffusely as total individuals." [3] Diffuseness is characteristic of *Gemeinschaft* conditions; specificity of *Gesellschaft*.

While *Gemeinschaft*, therefore, presupposes a sharing of fate, as both individuals and their community are treated as a totality, *Gesellschaft* presupposes a separateness of people between one relationship and the next; people are interested in people only one role at a time (father, business associate, commuter) and do not see others as total persons. This is the alienating part. On the other hand, Lipset is not the only writer to note that it is precisely this that is functional for liberal, moderate democracy. That is, in *Gesellschaft* the individual is like a small-scale pluralistic society, in which his many roles (like society's interest groups) balance against one another. Hence he can never be totally committed to one course, one extreme; extremist parties (and revolutionary politics) hold less attraction for him as other interests and roles compete to make him more moderate.

In the village this is not the case. The peasant tends to be conservative; that is, because his culture is one fabric, no part of it can really be changed without changing all. The parts are too interrelated, as are the roles that he plays as an individual.

As Mehmet Beqiraj points out: "As long as the social order of the peasantry seems to make ends meet . . . every social attitude is jealously preserved. Since the explanation of a particular phenomenon is possible only by reference to the entire order of phenomena . . . it follows that either the entire order . . . is religiously preserved as a whole, or it is all thrown overboard." [4] When one aspect of peasant society breaks down, reform cannot be achieved—it all breaks down. Thus the messianic movements of the peasants in fifteenth- and sixteenth-century Europe, or of tribalists in Melanesia, and thus the extreme, violent nature of peasant uprisings of all kinds. The *Gemeinschaft* rises together as one unit, as Frantz Fanon says.[5] Thus, too, the tendency to follow leaders or ideologies that promise total solutions (rather than merely reforms). Armed insurrection, often feared by the urban intellectual as undermining freedom, is taken more for granted as a form of struggle by the peasant, for whom freedom is meaningless without equality of the land.

This lack of understanding about "bourgeois civil liberties" carries over to the more oppressed strata of the urban proletariat, or sub-proletariat, for whom, as with the peasant, liberty is pointless without equality. Hence the frequent charges by Lipset and others about "working-class authoritarianism." But what is far more interesting for us is that at one extreme of the urban setting, a pseudo-*Gemeinschaft*, role-diffuse situation once again occurs. That is, on the one extreme we have the *Gemeinschaft* of the village. Then, with modernity and urbanization, we have the *Gesellschaft* of middle-class society, including the upper strata of the working class. But, at the other extreme, we have the unemployed and underemployed worker, and the unemployable under class, which, like the peasant villager, has fewer alternative roles to play that would tend toward a politics of moderation. The neighborhood becomes a pseudo-village, the fabric of life once more becomes closely meshed rather than segmented (because the individual, not working, spends all his time in the neighborhood, "on the street"); the "culture of poverty," insofar as it has value standards, acts in the same way as the poverty-culture of the village to create a role-diffuse individual.

This condition, then, leads to the modern "mass man," so often described in the literature of politics as vulnerable to totalitarian and extremist movements—like the peasant. Unlike middle-class man, whose many roles pluralistically offset each other, under-class man has only one role—to be sure, not that of village father-husband-agriculturalist and so on, but instead the diffuse role of poor black or white, for whom, when any aspect of life changes, all life changes at once. For under-class man, like the peasant, life is a constant crisis, totally dependent from day to day on fate.

The urban under class resembles the peasantry in another way: basically conservative so long as life is barely livable, in fact reactionary so far as politics is often concerned (infused, for example, with racism and a distrust of theory, cosmopolitan culture, and intellectualism), it catapults to revolutionism the moment life is no longer seen as livable for whatever reason. It has nothing to lose, only the world to gain, so why not?

Yet the classical urban revolution is not made by the under class or lumpenproletariat, which, in fact, has traditionally sided with reaction. The classical Marxian revolution is made by the industrial working class suffering some of the same conditions as the under class, but also infused with an ideology of democracy, socialism, trade unionism, with some degree of education, and with a more cosmopolitan, world-historical outlook which is the result of decades if not generations of literacy and working-class culture. It is precisely this class which has now joined, particularly in the United States, the middle class in its ideology, and which has therefore become largely non-, or anti-, revolutionary.

Today, in the developing world, it is no longer "possible to take seriously the view that the peasant is 'an object of history,' a form of social life over which historical changes pass but which contributes nothing to the impetus of these changes . . . the peasant in the modern era has been as much an agent of the revolution as the machine . . ." [6] The same thing is true of the urban under class. The urban working class, on the other hand, was always seen as an important lever for change, but seems to have become less so now. While it is true, therefore, that at a certain point either the peasantry or the pseudo-*Gemeinschaft* urban under class is capable of *making* a revolution, present historical evidence suggests that real power will accrue not to them but to the bureaucracy, the new class.

On whatever basis one chooses, then, whether it is on the nature of the peasantry, or that *plus* the need to have a democratic revolution, contemporary revolutionists claiming the Marxist label are not really Marxists at all. In different ways, they all represent rule by an elite, but they use Marxist language and peasant revolution (consciously or not) to justify their present or future rule. This may not be the intent, certainly, of Fanon, and perhaps not even of Guevara or General Giap, and perhaps not even of Debray, but it does seem to be the objective *function* of the contemporary peasant revolution and of its ideologies.

PEASANT REVOLUTIONISTS

Fanon is perhaps the most attractive, and also the least consistent, of these ideologues. Obviously a humane and cosmopolitan intellectual, he holds no brief for the post-independence elites who tend to be corrupt, who create situations in which the people "are silent, behave like a flock of sheep, and publish panegyrics in praise of the government or the leader." He understands that democracy consists of far more than "mobilizing three or four times a year ten thousand or a hundred thousand . . .," and that parties ought to be tools in the hands of the people. He sees the need for creating a large number of "well-informed nuclei at the bottom," but does not see how this is contradicted by the growth of an elite based on a peasant revolution.[7] He sees that the rural masses (in Algeria, for example) have revolutionary potential and are in fact more revolutionary than the bourgeoisified urban workers, and he castigates the revolutionary party for not educating the peasants sufficiently. But Fanon does not share the classical Marxian and sociological view that for peasants a democratic revolution is inherently an almost impossible achievement, given certain sociological rules about how elites work and how peasant life is organized. Finally, he sees violence as a "cleansing force," freeing the native from his inferiority complex; but he does not recognize that violence, when carried over into the post-independence period, itself creates forms of social life which undermine democracy. For the organization of violence, for whatever reason, is basically subversive of democratic values and institutions, and the habit of solving political issues through violent means, far from liberating, imprisons persons and personalities so that truly democratic participation in decision-making become nearly impossible. (See Chapter 3.)

So Fanon, while painfully aware of the problems confronting a peasant-based movement, and while fundamentally a democrat, does not really see how the peasant's inherent incapacity to rule society, plus the use of organized violence by the peasant revolutionary movement, no matter how necessary and inevitable, almost necessarily and inevitably leads the nation onto an elitist and authoritarian road.

For Guevara and Giap, as for Fanon, revolution is of the

peasant masses, organized into a liberation army. Their assumption, no matter how false, is that revolutionary politics creates for the revolutionary cadre a mass base in the countryside, and that politics, if relevant to the peasants' condition, will win "the hearts and minds of the people," to use a by now hackneyed phrase. Politics, then, precedes revolution, precedes military action against the imperialists or the native ruling class; military action flows out of political necessity and is dependent upon it. As Guevara says, "Where a government has come into power through some popular vote, fraudulent or not, and maintains at least an appearance of constitutional legality, the guerrilla outbreak cannot be promoted, since the possibilities of peaceful struggle have not yet been exhausted." For him, support by the people is the indispensable prerequisite for action. It is ironic to quote Guevara now: "This is clearly seen by considering the case of bandit gangs . . . They have all the characteristics of a guerrilla army . . . The only thing missing is support of the people; and, inevitably, these gangs are captured and exterminated by the public force." [8]

The view is shared by Mao Tse-tung: "Without a political goal, guerrilla warfare must fail, as it must fail if its political objectives do not coincide with the aspirations of the people . . ." [9] Mao is of course author of the famous phrase that guerrillas are like fish, and the people like the water. Giap, architect of the war against the French in Indo-China, likewise sees the need to "educate, mobilize, organize and arm the whole people" for the war of independence and revolution. [10] The problem of the land, he notes, is decisive, for "a people's war is essentially a peasants' war under the leadership of the working-class." Thus Giap turns on end Trotsky's slogan that a working-class revolution must be supported by the peasantry. "Under the leadership of the working-class" in circumstances where the cities are under foreign rule or are dictatorially controlled enclaves, really means "under the leadership of the party which says it acts for the working class," and that is another matter altogether.

But all of these particular ideologues for elitism, Fanon, Guevara, Giap, Mao, and others, agree that the process of liberation goes from political preparation of the countryside, to the insertion of guerrilla cadres into the countryside, to the formation of a guerrilla army, to the formation of a national liberation army, to victory. This was in fact the basic course of the Cuban revolution and the Chinese revolution, and it is the course of the Vietnam revolution—the working class, for whatever historical reason, had been defeated (as in China) or corrupted (as in Cuba and Algeria, with reservations) and played a secondary role. So the technicians of revolution took over in the name of the peasantry, and almost inevitably the iron law of oligarchy began to operate as it had in the Soviet Union many years before. The technicians of revolution became the new rulers of society.

Debray, however, breaks with even this nonconscious elitism and goes further. For him, Latin American conditions preclude the creation of large guerrilla base areas. He attacks Trotsky's conception of urban working-class insurrection as impossible for peasants under Latin American circumstances, mainly it seems because short-term insurrections will inevitably be suppressed. Guerrilla activity is, for Debray, a very long-range activity which *itself* creates the conditions for revolution—that is, it is not based necessarily on *prior* conditions. And so, obviously, premature insurrections in the cities are suppressed because the state is still able to function.[11] Well, Trotsky never suggested that revolutions ought to be attempted when the state is still stable; he did not seize power in Petrograd in 1914, which would have been a premature adventure, but only when conditions were ripe—after a disastrous war, in 1917. For Marxists, conditions cannot be manufactured by tiny elites. They must be developed so that revolutionary movements are responses *to* them. Debray's isolation and imprisonment in Bolivia testifies to his misunderstanding of that fact. As one observer dryly put it, "Recent history appears to indicate that mass movements without armed detachments simply invite official terror and repression; guerrilla detachments without mass movements are isolated, easily surrounded and overwhelmed by the Armed Forces." [12]

For Debray, "the guerrilla force is independent of the civilian population" so as to protect it from repression. Its *primary* task is to destroy the enemy's military potential. *Then* relations are established with the peasants. Propaganda, according to Debray, does not precede, it *follows* military activities by the guerrilla *focos* or centers. Initial propaganda is propaganda of the *deed*—for example, terrorism. So Debray's guerrilla band reverts historically to banditry, which is later followed by ideological work. To quote him, "armed propaganda follows military action . . . the most important form of propaganda is successful military action."

With Mao and Giap we have a mass revolution which, for sociological reasons, *leads* to elitism. With Debray we *begin* with elitism, that is, cadres of guerrillas who, later, in theory, let the peasants in on why they are being liberated. The ideology is to grow, spontaneously, from those who act. The city revolutionists, who are corrupt, must be subordinated to the countryside—the exact reverse of classical Marxist thinking and symptomatic of a profound disagreement about the values of urban and rural life: for Rosa Luxemburg or Trotsky the peasant is narrow; for Debray the worker is corrupt.

How is the goal of the revolution to be developed by Debray if military activity comes first, "excessive deliberation" is deemed a vice, and even the minimal democracy called "democratic centralism" by communists is too undisciplined?

If the guerrilla force is the party in embryo, what is the party to stand for? Here is where the existential, anti-Western Enlightenment aspect of the ruralites comes to full flower: it is the very nature of guerrilla warfare, a breeding ground of solidarity, comradeship, unity, brotherhood, *community* that *is* the ideology of Debray's revolution. It is, in short, *Gemeinschaft* we are after (which is an important key to understanding why certain alienated new leftists buy Debray's line, I think). It is no less than "a shedding of skin, a resurrection" that Debray is after. He admits it is a vision "a la Rousseau." It is also a vision after Hitler's Stormtroopers, as those familiar with Nazi literature, which so often talked of the "comradeship of the fighting front," will recognize.

It has been observed that Debray's view of revolutionary warfare fits into the Pentagon's view of insurgency and counter-insurgency warfare; the coincidence between Debray's views and those of W. W. Rostow is amazing—until one realizes that both are based on theories of change which minimize the role of the masses and see change as the work of tiny vanguards. It is interesting that often the very people who value the concept of community because they are alienated from the undemocratic nature of *Gesellschaft* life turn to methods and ideologies which lead to the organization of life along even more undemocratic lines.

This brings us to a final point on the quest for community. It is not only the guerrilla band which symbolizes community. It is peasant life as such, and in fact urban ghetto life as such, which seems to represent this—not for peasants or ghetto dwellers, who have no romantic illusions about their miserable condition. Rather, it is white, middle-class suburbanites of radical persuasion who romanticize peasant and ghetto life. They see all around them in the suburbs such a phony kind of community, feel such a sense of alienation, that they tend to align themselves theoretically with the peasants of this world. It's a kind of left-wing Goldwaterism, which sees the village or small town or ghetto neighborhood as virtuous, de-alienating, a town-meeting sort of place, and the city (or the suburb more specifically) as corrupt. This romanticism is not new: the Narodniki had it in czarist Russia, and college students in the 1930's who "went into factories" had similar illusions. If there is a sense of community in the peasant village, the price for it is abject poverty and the kind of alienation that comes of being a victim of climate and land-lords; if there is no community in the big city it is partly because nobody snoops into your affairs—they leave you alone. Where there is community in the big city it is a community of poverty and of fear. You pay your psychological money and take your cultural choice.

Views of revolution and of the nature of social class forces have always been colored, as have many other kinds of ideas about modern life, by people's underlying attitudes and values about the city and the country. It is, after all, one of the most profound ways of dividing men and nations, so it is not surprising that this basic conflict continues. In the same fashion, a critical issue is joined when one asks where change should be initiated—from above or from below? That, too, should not be a surprising conflict, for the issue of democracy versus elitism is constant in human affairs.

Of the revolutionary writers who have been mentioned, only Fanon and Rosa Luxemburg were basically democrats, and only Luxemburg [13] was urban-oriented. Lenin and Trotsky shared with modern peasant-oriented revolutionists a certain naiveté about sociological forces that tend to under-mine even the best intentions; it is with these forces that the next chapter will deal. Only Luxemburg, writing in 1919, seemed to grasp the basic fact that a revolutionary transfor-mation of society is not "something for which a ready-made formula lies completed in the pocket of the revolutionary party, which needs only to be carried out energetically in practice." On the contrary, socialism can only be "born out of the school of its own experience, born in the course of its realization." For her, democracy and participation were essential. "The whole mass of people must take part in it. Otherwise, socialism will be decreed from behind a few official desks by a dozen intellectuals . . ."

CHAPTER THREE

THE LIMITS
OF REVOLUTION

Several factors inhibit the democratic development of even an urban revolution: (1) problems of ideology inherent in all revolutionary *thought;* (2) problems of the revolutionary *personality;* and (3) problems of revolutionary *organization*. First, the tendency on the one hand to dominate action with ideology is subversive of democracy; on the other hand, the reverse is equally dangerous. Second, the kind of people who become active in insurrections and survive it *tend* not to be the kind of people who will create a positive, humanistic order; and third, the kind of organization seemingly required to conduct a violent effort is inherently subversive of such an order. To put it into a sort of folk saying (if Barrington Moore will forgive me): ". . . it is a good working rule to be suspicious about political and intellectual leaders who talk mainly about moral values; many poor devils are liable to be badly hurt." [1]

Norman Mailer is not the first to note a profound distinction between the Old American Left and the New Left: the Old Left, whether communist, Trotskyist, or socialist, proceeded, and proceeds, in a deductive fashion, always detailing "the sound-as-brickwork logic in the next step in some new . . . program." The New Left induces from its experience "that you created the revolution first and learned from it, learned of what your revolution might consist and where it might go out of the intimate truth of the way it presented itself to your experience." For the traditional, Marxist left, understanding and analysis, plan and program precede action and revolution; for the new, Freudian-Marxist revolutionists, the idea is "of a revolution which preceded ideology," so that day-to-day practice creates the ideology, inductively.[2]

For the radical, the relationship between action and ideology is always the most difficult of all problems; especially so, then, when it comes to trying to plan the form of the culmination, the terminal point of radical action, the revolution itself. There is no easy solution. For a real radical, this is a dialectical struggle in which program and practice constantly affect one another, leading to the development and, hopefully, progress of the movement. In one way, it is a struggle to be welcomed because of its very difficulty, because it insures that the program will be real and at the same time that practice will not simply be based on momentary whim or opportunity. It is a struggle to be welcomed, as well, because it insures the *democratic* development of the movement as the program is hammered out in day-to-day confrontation with the practical needs of the masses who are, in theory, to be involved in their own emancipation.

One aspect of the history of radicalism is the history of this struggle as it takes place in the context of specific social and economic conditions. Too much emphasis on the immediate, on practice, and the goals are lost sight of; the movement, because it has no program, often becomes social-democratic, liberal, a tool of the status quo, led by "betrayers." Too much emphasis on program and the movement becomes isolated, sectarian, populated by adventurers, and profoundly elitist as it substitutes fancy blueprints for programs that are developed in the course of interaction with the system, the problems it creates, and the people it disaffects.

It is in particularly difficult and frustrating times, when the masses with whom radicals interact are not on the move, as in the United States, or are frightened into apathy, as sometimes in Latin America, that the utopian or left-wing adventuristic tendencies so neatly described in Lenin's *Left-Wing Communism, An Infantile Disorder,* appear strongest. Lacking faith in the masses' moving on their own behalf, such radicals often take into their own hands the decisions as to what is best for others, and so make plans, create utopias, and even seek violent short-cuts to change in the face of apathy.

But for a real radical such short-cuts are not a solution because they create more problems than they solve, divert energies from the development of the movement, and, most important of all, turn the movement into elitist, anti-democratic directions. Why is the utopian tendency elitist? Because, as Marx said in the *Communist Manifesto,* "Historical action is to yield to their [the utopians'] personal inventive action, historically created conditions of emancipation to fantastic ones, and the gradual, spontaneous class-organization of the proletariat to an organization of society specially contrived by these inventors. Future history resolves itself, in their eyes, into the propaganda and the practical carrying out of their social plans."

Just as it is true for radicalism in general that the revolutionary program should develop from struggle but also be informed by history and theory, so it is true for the insurrectionary movement. Neither an insurrection initiated with pre-conceived ideas nor one which negates the role of ideas can have a democratic outcome—apart from obstacles to democracy inherent in paramilitary organizational structure. The trouble is that in violent times the apparent "payoffs" for short-cuts are the highest; violence and elitism fit together very nicely.

THE MYSTIQUE OF ACTION

It is not necessary to have a plan in order to be an elitist. The movement that has no program tends, as I have said, to opportunism, and that too is elitist. But opportunists rarely make insurrections, so we are not really concerned with that facet of the left. Debray is an elitist not because he is an opportunist, nor because he has a plan. He is an elitist because he proposes to exclude the masses from decision-making over the revolutionary movement until, by some mystical process, the guerrilla band decides the masses are ready. At this point, somehow, the program will develop out of action.

This view is related to Debray's basic attitude toward the importance of ideas and rationality as against feeling and action—another way of saying the urban tradition against the rural, or, in one sense, Marx versus Marcuse. The party-less, program-less movement of action (labeled by some "confrontation politics") is related, therefore, to the *Gemeinschaft* concept common to those pro-peasant views outlined in the previous chapter. Moore, for example, describes the "Catonic" view of peasant life, the denigration of rational analysis characteristic of the peasant mystique.[3] Bertrand Russell attacks D. H. Lawrence's approach, which is closely related, terming it "thinking with the blood," and arguing that this denial of the intellect "led straight to Auschwitz."

This issue has become one of the divisive generational factors in the American left. There are some, particularly those "over thirty," who are bound by the traditions of linear, rational thinking which involves a concern for the consequences of action, no matter how moral actions may seem in themselves. There are others for whom action, love, feeling, expression are important in themselves, a kind of existential reaction to an overly rationalized and technological society. For these, Debray's mystique of action holds a certain attraction; they share his mistrust of conventional political ideologies. On the American scene, the incessant betrayals and seeming betrayals by so-called liberals and socialists of their announced aspirations seems more than adequate evidence of the futility of theories and ideologies for many alienated students and desperate ghetto blacks. For them, one action is worth a thousand words, and the Marcusian admonition to drop out so you can't cop out falls on eager ears.

It is not surprising, therefore, that Herbert Marcuse suggests that the only really revolutionary class consists of "the outcasts and outsiders, the exploited and persecuted of other races and other colors, the unemployed and the unemployable . . . [who] exist outside the democratic process . . ." [4] This is precisely that under class which I discussed in the previous chapter in terms of "pseudo-*Gemeinschaft*," that element most susceptible to total revolution, to "thinking with the blood." We have, then, a strange alliance between humanistic politics and the worship of those less rational bases of politics which have traditionally been the source of support for . . . fascism.

Denigration of rational thought and worship of action has led, historically, to worship of violence and the concept of violence as a therapeutic force. For the traditional Marxist, violence was always a dependent variable, a tool, a tactic to be used under certain limited historical circumstances, usually in defense against violence mounted against a workers' movement by counter-revolutionary elements. At best it was tragic. But with the rise of revolutionary independence movements

in the Third World, and with the failure of non-violent movements in American race relations, violence has once again
become respectable, even a mark of prestige in left-wing
circles. Guevara, Fanon, and Debray have become New Left
heroes, and Sartre and D. H. Lawrence have replaced Rosa
Luxemburg and Lenin as patron saints of revolution. Violence
has become, in short, an independent variable, and the same
circumstances that create an alliance between humanism and
the denigration of thought also lead to frightening conver-
gences between motorcycle gangs and Stormtroopers, and
between Fanon's mystique of violence and the attack on
Western Enlightenment by Hitlerism and its philosophical
antecedents. The worship of action for the sake of action, the
support of feeling over rational thought, the generalized attack
on the Western tradition (as opposed to the Marxian attack
on specific aspects of Western thought), often encountered
in the ranks of hippiedom and some black nationalism and
New Leftism, cannot help but remind those over thirty of
some of these sentiments:

> Fascism is, above all, action and sentiment and that it
> must continue to be . . . Only because it is feeling and
> sentiment, only because it is the unconscious reawaken-
> ing of our profound racial instinct, has it the force to
> stir the soul of a people . . .[5]

> National socialism is action pure and simple, dynamics
> *in vacuo* . . . one thing it is not—doctrine or philosophy.[6]
> Fascism has not been wholly successful with the intel-
> lectual classes (because of the fixity of their acquired
> rational culture) . . . it has been very successful with
> young people, with women, in rural districts, and among
> men of action unencumbered by a fixed and set social
> and political education.[7]

These are precisely the alienated, marginal elements of society which have been shown to form the backbone of the "radical right," and in some respects also of the non-traditional left, particularly that element which seems to be gravitating to the guerrilla mystique.

The quest for community in the form of the fighting group, which is seen as being the ultimate in comradeship and romance, is related to the worship of violence. So is the Latin American concept of *machismo,* or manliness. As Irving Louis Horowitz recently pointed out, the guerrilla mystique is the incarnation of "virility in speech, action, and dress, virility expressed by bravado, courage, and ruthlessness," precisely those qualities denied, for example, the black male by American society.[8] For the young ghetto black, paramilitary posturing may soon replace the juvenile fighting gang as his way of finding the masculinity denied him by white society. The same thing would be true of young men in the oppressed sectors of the world—it is an idea closely related to Fanon's concept of violence as a psychologically liberating force, so that it is no wonder that Fanon has been so avidly read by opponents of non-violence in the civil rights movement. Violence, according to Fanon, is potent, virile—non-violence is castrating. Of course, we should remember that there is no clinical evidence one way or the other except Fanon's own cases, which are somewhat contradictory. And sociological evidence would seem to point strongly to the conclusion that even if violence occasionally is cathartic for the individual, at the same time it undermines the creation of anything approaching a "therapeutic community," if by that we mean a humanistically oriented community of brotherhood.

Violence, for one thing, is a symptom of bitterness and frustration when it takes political form. For certain alienated groups in this and other societies, violence is seen as the only remaining device, the only device that is not co-optable, in a situation where all other measures have failed. It is for this reason that Fanon sees violence as cleansing and that Debray distrusts even radical political parties—all else results in betrayal. Only violence can lead to what is, in a way, a "final solution." The same situation applies to many younger urban blacks—"better to die on your feet than live on your knees." But this is a solution which by definition precludes a plan for the future, much less a democratic one. Once one has accepted a solution by suicide, one has already stopped discussing the "means-ends" problem.

The problem of ideology is that overplanning leads to separation from the masses, hence to elitism; underplanning leads either to opportunism or to thinking-by-feeling, hence to the kind of movement that denies the valid contributions of the Western Enlightenment. Even worse, an ideology of action for-the-sake-of-action tends to glorify violence for its own sake: both in terms of personality and organization, violence, far from being therapeutic, endangers when it does not utterly destroy the humanistic component of a social movement.

THE REVOLUTIONARY PERSONALITY

Fanon was not the first to point out that oppressed people, frustrated and unable to focus their discontent in a political fashion, frequently aggress against each other (in-group hostility) or engage in various kinds of cathartic motor behavior in which their violent feelings in some way find means of harmless expression (dancing, religious possession, and so forth). That is, if aggression against the true source of oppression is excluded because it would mean instant retaliation and death, aggression must take place in some other way. Rioting, even though the oppressed group ends up as chief victim, serves a similar function although it is politically one step more advanced: "American Negro rioters . . . seem to share one basic psychological dynamic with striking French farmers, Guatemalan guerrillas, and rioting Indonesian students: most of them feel frustrated in the pursuit of their goals, they are angered as a consequence, and because of their immediate social circumstances they feel free enough, or desperate enough, to act on that anger." [9]

Once the historical stage of in-group aggression (high murder rates, for example both in the American ghetto and in Algeria), religious ecstasy, and rioting has passed, violence takes the form of various kinds of paramilitary activity, including terrorism. It may involve a mass revolutionary movement, in which case, according to Fanon, violence serves the function of unifying the people, of nation-building.[10] For the individual, it "is a cleansing force. It frees the native from his inferiority complex and from his despair and inaction; it makes him fearless and *restores his self-respect*" (my emphasis).

The story is confirmed by various observers. Recounts a member of the Nazi party, ". . . I recovered the exhilarating sense of comradery I had known in the army"; said another, "We were united by the terrorism raging around us;" a third, ". . . I always felt happy to see the little groups of brown-clad soldiers march through the city with rhythmic strides and straightforward mien." [11] Says Eldridge Cleaver, upon first seeing members of the Black Panther Party for Self-Defense, "I . . . saw the most beautiful sight I had ever seen: four black men wearing black berets, powder-blue shirts, black leather jackets, black trousers . . . and each with a gun!" [12] Similar sentiments have come from others, for example immigrants or Jewish visitors to Israel upon first seeing Israeli soldiers.

The question should, however, be raised as to whether this therapeutic effect stems from violence or from the effect of struggling against oppression, regardless of violent or non-violent content. The argument has been made by a number of authors, among others Reverend Martin Luther King, Jr. (in various writings and speeches), that the fact of fighting for one's rights non-violently is therapeutic also—it is, then, standing up that counts, not standing up with gun in hand. Compare, for example, this statement from Nehru, describing a non-violent campaign, with those just quoted: ". . . we had a sense of freedom and a pride in that freedom. The old feeling of oppression and frustration was completely gone . . . We had . . . an agreeable sense of moral superiority over our opponents, in regard to both our goals and our methods . . ." [13]

The negative consequences of violence for the health of the personality also must be mentioned, even though in many ways they should by now be obvious. Fanon's cases, cited in the closing section of *The Wretched of the Earth,* in fact refute his arguments as to the therapy of violence in many instances. The internal conflict over orders to kill, resulting in psychiatric disturbances, has been noted in populations ranging from concentration camp guards to American GI's. And structural consequences must be noted with those to the individual: the losses to society of the skills of those killed or exiled, the setbacks in economic growth, the acute losses of population (perhaps 150,000 in the Algerian War), the undermining of social structures such as family, village, and community, and, of course, the dangers to the society of the future, originating in the violent strategies of the past. B. H. Liddell Hart observes how even effective guerrilla campaigns such as those in Spain against Napoleon were "followed by an epidemic of armed revolutions that continued in quick succession for half a century . . ." [14]

Violence, therefore, is of questionable value in creating a liberating personality. Furthermore, because it is illegal and dangerous, it attracts a different kind of person than is attracted to a conventional reform movement. The underground figure is dedicated and self-sacrificing; prison is an honor, a proof of trust, of great political value after the revolution. But the high level of motivation required in such endeavors implies an unusual personality, a deviant (because tiny minority) type. Nechayev describes him: "The revolutionist is a doomed man. He has no personal interests, no affairs, sentiments, attachments, property, not even a name of his own. Everything in him is absorbed by one exclusive interest, one thought, one passion—the revolution." [15] Not all revolutionists go to Gandhi's extreme, that of taking the vow of celibacy, but one cannot help but shudder at least slightly at the thought of the humorless type described by Nechayev ruling post-revolutionary society. "On the New Left, too, among all these young Dantons, Desmoulins, Marats of fantasy and possibility, one can already pick out here and there the tight-lipped manner, the careful dress, and the touch of pedantry of the potential Robespierre. The play-actors have returned to the stage, but the Puritans are waiting their turn." [16]

One can go further. As one military observer has noted, "the heaviest handicap of all, and the most lasting one, was of a moral kind. The armed resistance movement [of the European undergrounds] attracted many 'bad-hats.' It gave them license to indulge their vices and work off their grudges under the cloak of patriotism . . . This left a disrespect for 'law and order' that inevitably continued after the invaders had gone." [17] The release of aggression sanctioned by revolution, that release deemed therapeutic by Fanon, is not therapeutic in the society after a revolution. This feeling that violence is sanctioned simply does not disappear when the revolution is over; as J. K. Zawodny puts it, "No political leadership can satisfy all aspirations of guerrillas . . . consequently, each movement relying on violence contains a potential seed of future counter-revolution in those of its own rank and file who emerge from the struggle dissatisfied and who are *conditioned to use violence as a means for solving their problems*" (my emphasis).[18]

This particular aspect of revolutionary struggle is sometimes termed "the principle of the transfer of total opposition." It works this way: Before the revolution any opposition to a totalitarian or authoritarian regime (for example, a colonial power) is considered by the regime to be subversive by definition; hence any opposition must be total opposition, prepared for prison, exile, and, hopefully, ultimately revolution. The politics of absolute opposition imposed by a police state leads to the disappearance of all middle-of-the-roaders. "The symbol 'compromise' enjoys a bad reputation, almost on a par with 'opportunism.' " [19] Compromisers are therefore perceived as betrayers. When independence or liberation is achieved, the moderates are dealt with; objectively, they had sided with the enemy. The new rulers, cloaked with the mantle of revolutionary legitimacy, are the only possible rulers—by definition those who did not participate, those who are not with the rulers, are excluded. But the rulers often end up disagreeing, especially where there are latent conflicts among various strata in the population as to how the power is to be divided. Those who go into opposition thereby separate themselves from revolutionary legitimacy and are treated as if they were counter-revolutionaries, in league with those who have just been replaced. If opposition is to be maintained, it must be outside of legitimate channels, which are monopolized by the new government; so that any new opposition becomes revolutionary in turn. All other avenues being closed to it, the new opposition is left with no alternative than to make another revolution, to take up arms against the state it had helped to create.

THE REVOLUTIONARY ORGANIZATION

This principle of the transfer of total opposition is related to the form of organization used by a movement in the pre-revolutionary period, including its organization of violence. Sociological studies of complex organizations have often made the point that the most idealistic goals tend to be undermined by the organizations set up to achieve those goals, or simply, that the ends are implied in the means, or that the ends do not justify the means because the means change the ends.

This is even more true of revolutionary movements which, whether they will it or not, must protect themselves against repression in a police state society. Doing so, they emulate the police state, building structures that maximize security precautions.

A revolution is a war; a revolutionary organization must therefore be military in nature. It is endangered constantly by spies and provocateurs. It must be able to make decisions quickly and have them carried out without question; it cannot, therefore, permit lengthy discussions and debates, or loose organization without a clear-cut chain of command. It must prevent the enemy from uncovering the whole operation if one part of it is uncovered; therefore, only small teams are safe, and the less people know, the better. Such an organization is the very antithesis of democracy. People trained in it, and comfortable within its confines, cannot, no matter how ardently they try, create a humanistic society. It was for this reason that Moses was only permitted to see, but not enter, the Promised Land.

What is particularly odious about the revolutionary organization is the constant fear that many of the participants justifiably must have of infiltrators and informers. Secret societies are made to order for the police in an interesting way: they enable the police to justify their own existence. The line is by now familiar, especially when it comes to asking for increased budgets: "The threat from subversive elements is great and we are doing a lot to solve the problem." (Hence, a few arrests and trials.) "But the problem is still very large." (Unprovable, since measures taken are secret.) "Therefore we need still more funds and facilities."

For the revolutionary organization as for democratic society, suspicion of informers, whether based on reality or not, poisons the atmosphere. It undermines such discussion as may exist and therefore promotes the further subversion of the organization's democratic procedures, however limited they may be. The danger from provocation is always present, so every person's credentials are constantly under scrutiny. "Does he advocate this or that because this would be exactly what the police would like, or not?"

A revolutionary organization operating clandestinely is also open to a counter-measure called the "pseudo-gang." [20] This is an operation in which the government recruits a group to *pose* as an independent revolutionary organization. This group then carries out several illegal acts and is contacted by the regular underground which seeks an alliance or some degree of control or coordination with it. Thus the government obtains, through the pseudo-gang, valuable information about the real illicit organization. Sometimes the pseudo-gang is absorbed into the regular organization, thus saturating it with informers. Rumors concerning possible pseudo-gangs of ultra-militant black nationalists have, in fact, already begun to circulate in the United States.

The secret organization's vulnerability to police agents, provocation, and entrapment, is easy to see. In the spring of 1968 a New York City detective testified how he had infiltrated the Revolutionary Action Movement, a black nationalist group, and become a member of a three-man terrorist cell that was to murder several prominent moderate civil rights leaders. He had himself played a part in the alleged conspiracy, so that the police department had, in effect, assisted the plot. It was his word against the defendants'. They were convicted. Secret societies are made to order for that kind of "set-up," and really have no way of protecting themselves against it.

The only form of revolutionary organization not susceptible to this basic disease is the non-violent one, in which the revolution need not have a military organization because, first of all, it does not need to organize violence, and, second, because it has no secrets (thereby openly accepting repression). By its very nature ". . . non-violence is inherently a democratizing influence. For learning the techniques and philosophy of non-violence means that (the participant) must become intimately involved with his subject, hence must become deeply aware of himself, of the people who work with him and against him, and of his environment. Such an awareness on the part of large numbers . . . precludes or at least sharply limits the development of narrow elites." [21] Non-violence works best when large numbers participate. In order to motivate them, given the high risks involved, serious education must take place. In a sense, a *Gemeinschaft* or community must be created in which the non-violent practitioner is far more involved as a person than would be the case for a violent practitioner. The latter's role is often far more limited in the total picture (for example, he may only store ammunition in his cellar), so his motivation can also be more limited. Violence, in short, does not require either large numbers or as deep a commitment: it depends on the task. Non-violence requires commitment regardless of task, for all tasks are risky, thus education is essential.

In summary, the types of personalities, as well as the forms of organization, that usually emerge in a violent revolutionary struggle, regardless of its level (coup, terrorism, guerrilla warfare, or urban revolution), are those which undercut the humanistic hopes of such endeavors. Violent transitions of power, unhappily, make for conditions in which the "transfer of total opposition principle" works out so that the violent conditions of struggle before the revolution carry over and hamper the task of reconstruction. This seems to be true not only for movements which in any case are elitist-oriented— although it will be worse in conditions where there is no consciousness of this problem, or where, indeed the very raising of the issue is considered subversive (as in many Communist parties); [22] it is true, alas, for even the most benign, consciously motivated, humanistically inclined movements. The problem can be partially offset, perhaps balanced, by trying to build in democratic mechanisms, but so far in history no movement has managed successfully to solve it. Some kind of Thermidorean reaction [23] has always set in, and somehow, following a violent revolution or uprising, some of the survivors always end up standing in the rubble asking, "Is this what we did it for?" and "Was it worth it?" History cannot unmake revolutions, and such questions can never be answered.

CHAPTER FOUR

PARAMILITARY ACTIVITIES IN URBAN AREAS

Urban insurrections and other forms of urban political violence by definition are historically more advanced forms of collective protest than such pre- or proto-political forms as gangsterism, rioting, or looting.[1] Insurrections may be either *defensive* (oriented to the violent defense of some existing system against the encroachments of some force, usually from the outside, as in the case of the Paris Commune) or *offensive* (against the existing system of government, as in the case of revolutionary outbreaks), although the distinction is rarely a neat one. (A ghetto uprising, as in Warsaw or Harlem, has both defensive and offensive implications.)

TERRORISM

One of the handiest ways of classifying and discussing urban political violence is to look at the numerical component: how many people are involved? Is it a mass movement or an elitist, vanguard-oriented movement? (The basic distinction is that made in Chapter 1, between urban terrorism and the urban rebellion or "rising.") We can logically begin this discussion with individual acts of terrorism (including sniping), directed against people, and sabotage, directed against property or material symbols. Individual violence such as terrorism and sabotage may indicate the weakness of a movement, representing the work of a desperate few; or it may represent only the first stage of a growing movement, remaining an important adjunct of, say, a larger underground or resistance movement later. Terrorism and sabotage can be directed either against purely military objectives (normally the case in a defensive strategy) or toward a more profound subversion of the government. It can be discriminating in its victims or indiscriminate in its violence; either method can be part of a primarily military (defensive) or a primarily subversive (offensive) strategy, depending largely on degree.

Subversion need not be violent. Disruptive tactics to undermine the functioning of the goverment can be and often are non-violent or a-violent. They can including tying up government offices with false accusations or letter-writing campaigns or phone calls, botching up industrial production with forged communications, overloading the system by turning in false alarms, slow-down campaigns at the work place, malingering, switching street signs, overuse of and overconformity to regulations (the "good soldier Schweik" system), and the like.

One possible objective of terrorism is to make repression of it so costly that a government (for example, in a colonial setting) prefers withdrawal to continued occupation. Indiscriminate terrorism tends to be more disruptive; discriminate terrorism more politically symbolic and oriented to gaining allies rather than discouraging an occupying power. It may even be motivated primarily by the calculation that counter-terror will be provoked, hence allies from among the victims of the government's (likely indiscriminate) repression can be gained. This has been the case more often than not.

Terrorism, therefore, is often merely an entering wedge, and it can be effectively used to build a larger movement even by a very small vanguard. Terrorism and sabotage, especially when combated by a government using repression and counter-terror (for example, taking and shooting hostages), can create a movement where none existed before. Above all, terrorism can lead to the subversion of the social base of the society, as happened during the German Weimar Republic, when "Violence was employed primarily to alter certain of the conventions of the society in such a way as to make a republican form of government inappropriate to it, rather than in the hope of direct capture of the state . . ." [2] By the use of street brawling, beatings, and assassinations, the Nazi party discredited "argument and compromise as political means" and transferred political decision-making from the parliamentary environment to the streets. In short, it was not freedom of speech that brought the Nazis to power—it was freedom to perform illegal acts of subversion without significant punishment, and often with the tacit consent of a rightist police force.

Contemporary analogies, both right and left, are obvious. The attempt to transfer political decision-making from bureaucracies, which are seen as ineffective or corrupt, or as agents of a foreign power, to other groups whose participation is considered somehow more legitimate, is in itself a neutral category. It becomes revolutionary or counter-revolutionary depending on what group is seen as the legitimate alternative to current power-holders. The political state, and its arm the police force, is supposedly the neutral protector of the current power structure against the encroachments of both left and right when they exceed the bounds of legality. But in reality this neutrality almost inevitably bends to the side of the right, which the power structure and especially its police arm prefers to the left. This is partially so because the police are more conservative than the state itself (and at times are in conflict with it, as over the issue of the rights of criminals); the social and psychological make-up of the police (very often lower middle class, and racist, in the United States particularly) assures that.

The dangers of terrorism to a revolutionary movement, including the psychological and structural dangers mentioned in the preceding chapter, should be kept in mind. An eleven-page mimeographed article advocating sabotage as the "next logical step toward obstruction and disruption of the U.S. war machine" provides an example. The article, written in 1967 and of course unsigned, gives Toronto as its origin. The article was picked up by the mass media and used to smear the peace movement as subversive, resulting in needless allocation of resources within the movement to disavow the strategy of sabotage. The question as to whether the article was "genuine" or a deliberate plant or provocation was also raised—it may have been either, demonstrating once more how easy it is for opponents to create problems by such means in a movement which is not totally and clearly non-violent.

The Toronto article only advocated sabotage; the failure of the American anti-war movement to end the war in Vietnam by ordinary means has already resulted in the fact of sabotage. According to William Worthy, writing in the *Boston Globe,* at least eight bombings and burnings of Selective Service or military facilities had occurred in the United States by the end of July 1968. "Because all the organized peace groups have been thoroughly infiltrated by government agents, the *successful* acts of sabotage will be carried out by single individuals and by small intimate groups of long-time friends," says Worthy, in predicting more such activity.[3] This is indeed the pattern of successful, early-stage underground activity.

Either left or right can create subversive conditions, and if they are not impartially suppressed these conditions can become serious. It should therefore not be surprising that the Columbia University disturbances in the spring of 1968 excited vigorous police repression, and that the assassination of Senator Robert Kennedy in turn was attributed by some people to the atmosphere of lawlessness promoted by some student groups. In the sense that both acts were subversive, such observers were superficially correct. But it must be remembered that the students' subversion was diametrically opposed to the assassin's subversion—it was anti-bourgeois from the left (note its seizure of *property*) rather than anti-bourgeois from the *right*. It is interesting that leftists are often blamed for the incursions of the right on the democratic process, whereas the ultra-right (for example, the Minutemen, the Klan) are rarely blamed for "creating an atmosphere of violence" when leftists act illegally. Rightists are sometimes suppressed, while leftists are more often prosecuted; if Minutemen and Klansmen were given the same police treatment the Black Panthers get, there probably would be no Minutemen.

It is possible, then, for terrorism and sabotage, as used by a small underground band or secret society, to create conditions in which many normal functions of the society can no longer be effectively carried out. The government tends to overreact, or underreact; when it overreacts it has the freedom to retreat, hence pose as generous. When it underreacts it has the freedom to entrap and provoke the underground to show its hand prematurely and be destroyed. But there are limits. Overreaction is often interpreted by the population as panic; underreaction as ignorance of the real situation, or softness, hence both reactions can play into the hands of the terrorists.[4]

The terrorist or saboteur does not necessarily intend revolution. He *may,* feeling that terrorism is only the first step in that direction. But more often he only wants to remove a specific evil (the Vietnam War, police brutality, alleged communist influence in a community) or a specific evil person. This is particularly so when the terrorist is acting on his own, without any wider conspiracy, as with many assassinations of public officials. One can say, in fact, that the ultimate intent of the terrorist can be twisted to the requirements of the government, so that in some ways terrorism can strengthen a regime. For example, an individual act can be made to appear as if it were a conspiracy, so that the government can use it as an excuse for various kinds of repression against dissident groups. Contrariwise, the government can try to make a conspiracy look like the act of a demented individual in order (a) to protect some of its own people who may have been involved or (b) to protect a social myth which says the society is basically healthy; a conspiracy is proof that something is amiss.

THE UNDERGROUND

As a terrorism-and-sabotage group becomes a larger-scale underground movement (possibly part of a wider resistance movement including guerrillas), its opportunities to subvert the society become correspondingly greater. The individual assassin may join a secret society (the Decembrists, the Carbonarii, the Molly Maguires, and so forth), and this rather narrowly based proto-revolutionary formation may then move toward becoming a junta (a military conspiracy, from the top) or a mass resistance or revolutionary movement (from the bottom, like the Irish Republican Army); or it may even develop into a legitimate trade union or political party.[5]

An underground, defined technically, consists of "clandestine organizational elements of politico-military movements attempting to illegally weaken, modify, or replace an existing governing authority." [6] By implication, then, an underground is usually a part of a wider *resistance* movement (referring to the kind made famous during World War II, dedicated simply to restoring the status quo ante bellum), or *revolutionary* movement (referring to an effort to overthrow a domestically originated government). In either case, the underground is usually linked to other elements, such as guerrilla bands, and forms its "internal supply arm." Members of an underground "usually play legal roles within society, with their underground membership concealed." The underground, as a supply arm, "buys supplies on the black market . . . may steal goods from warehouses, or conduct open raids to get supplies. Sometimes undergrounds manufacture weapons and ammunition . . ." In this kind of a situation, there may be "for every guerrilla member of a revolutionary movement . . . two to twenty-seven underground members." [7] But resistance or revolutionary movements may also begin underground without any wider connections to other elements, at least initially. Many are, in fact, suppressed at that stage, or remain simple underground conspiracies with minor acts of terror or sabotage for many years. Their chief reason for existence may be illegal propaganda work and self-education (as under the Czar).

The underground movement cannot survive "ad infinitum; a terminal point of struggle must be indicated . . . hopeless struggle can scarcely attract a large following." [8] The closer victory appears, the larger the following; the more distant the terminal point, the smaller the following—and as it becomes larger, victory indeed comes closer. Conversely, as the movement becomes smaller it is often doomed to defeat, or to a long wait until somehow the cycle can be reversed by new historical circumstances. Sooner or later, then, a resistance movement must attempt a revolution (or be liberated by an outside army, for which it can play an important auxiliary role) or face failure. To remain "contained" for a long time is equivalent to failure. "La guerre" becomes "fini." For that reason, in desperation some underground movements occasionally lash out with a wave of terrorism and thereby are rescued (or finally defeated in one spasmodic episode). For that reason, too, they are susceptible to provocation and to agents provocateurs.

Among the more successful resistance movements, in the sense that they culminated in an overthrow of government, were those in western Europe in World War II, in central and eastern Europe after World War II, and a tiny handful of others such as in Palestine under Great Britain, and in Ireland. But "more successful" is a relative term; in both the Irish and Israeli situations the occupying power was involved in a difficult international situation at the time, and, while both were largely independent and unaided efforts, they were in a real sense nationwide revolutions with at least some outside sympathy and attention, so that the occupying power was limited in the amount of repression it felt able to use.

The communist seizures of power in central and eastern Europe, notably in Czechoslovakia in 1948, were not popular insurrections in the normal sense. Typically, the communists, supported by the presence of Soviet troops, were already part of a coalition government and had infiltrated the military organs of the government. In Prague, in 1948, the process of taking over lasted five days. The police were already communist-controlled, and the army was paralyzed by communist influence and Soviet restrictions. Diplomatic pressure was also brought to bear; it was hardly a clear-cut case for "internal war." [9]

One measure of success, at least for a resistance movement linked to a wider war, is the help such a movement can give to the regular armed forces (as in World War II). The ability of an underground to tie up enemy troops is proven: when the British withdrew from Palestine, the combined resistance forces of the Haganah, the Irgun, and the Stern Gang had tied up three divisions, several R.A.F. squadrons, 7,400 soldiers of the Arab Legion, 3,000 members of the Trans-jordanian Frontier Force, 4,000 British members of the Palestine Police Force, "plus the Mediterranean Fleet." [10] The contribution made by the Israelis to Gandhi's non-violent movement by preventing some British troops from going to India has not been fully evaluated.

Similarly, in Italy in World War II, the partisan movement (including both underground and guerrilla elements) gradually became so large that the Germans were forced to launch offensive after offensive against it; the partisans took heavy losses and "the most ferocious massacres of the civilian population [were] accompanied by the ever-more frequent reconquest of the partisan zones . . . [this] culminated in the horrifying slaughter of Marzabotto [1,830 civilians massacred between the 29th of September and the 1st of October 1944]." [11] Despite such setbacks, partisans continued active and on occasion even broke through the lines to fight with Allied troops. "The Resistance had succeeded in transforming itself into an organized popular insurrection," so much so that ultimately a treaty setting forth its relationship to the Allies was drawn up. The Italian Resistance included about a quarter-million actual soldiers, of whom some 45,000 died in battle. They were largely supplied by the Allies, who dropped some eight hundred tons of goods to them between May and August 1944, and over twelve hundred tons during the last four months of the war.

In France a similar picture developed after the Allied landings. "The enemy," said Supreme Allied Headquarters, "was facing a battlefield behind his lines." The French Forces of the Interior had, by August 1944, grown to 100,000 armed troops. [12]

Such large-scale campaigns, however, do not make a clear-cut case for the viability of insurrections in a modern urban setting. While defensive insurrections almost always are able to secure more popular support than offensive ones, "Probably all students of partisan warfare are agreed that the partisan contribution to the outcome of World War II was not decisive. . . . Yet there is no doubt that on the whole the partisans gave valuable assistance to the Allied armies." [13] The undergrounds were also useful in gathering intelligence. Some of their sabotage was severe, and they liberated several cities (Antwerp, Paris) in advance of oncoming Allied troops. Generally, though, they remained subordinate to outside military activity.

Even under the most difficult conditions, however, including lack of popular support, undergrounds did exist and survive. The classic case is that of Germany itself during World War II. As late as 1940 a group of Berlin communists managed to publish the official newspaper of the party. Clandestine contacts took place throughout the war between Soviet prisoners of war and German underground groups, and as late as April-May 1944 a German underground publication in French made its way to French prisoners and internees. And there was, of course, the terrorist plot to assassinate Hitler in June 1944. But the cost of this activity was extremely high: in the years 1942, 1943, and 1944 there were 14,841 *official* (reported) executions of German resistance workers by the Reich Ministry of Justice. Army records indicate that, in addition, 24,559 soldiers were executed between August 16, 1939, and January 31, 1945, for various causes. These figures do not include vast numbers who died in concentration camps. In Austria, too, an underground existed under most severe conditions. Over 2,700 Austrians were executed specifically for resistance activities (again, not including perhaps 182,000 Austrians killed in concentration camps for related religious, political, or ethnic activities).[14]

The case of the Netherlands illustrates some of the problems faced by an underground movement in modern, chiefly urban, conditions. In Holland there were few places German occupying soldiers could not reach in a hurry. The nation, with a high population density, has few woods, no mountains—"no country could be imagined offering less possibilities for guerrilla warfare . . ." [15] Even sea and air communication with the Allies was difficult—the coast was blockaded. There were no contiguous borders with neutral nations for purposes of smuggling. The German air defense system permeated the Dutch countryside. Furthermore, the Germans behaved somewhat more correctly in Holland than elsewhere, due to the importance of Dutch agricultural production to the German population. Hence the first anti-German political murder did not take place until 1943, and non-violent resistance ("civilian defense") was more prevalent.

Civilian resistance took the form of strikes at first. At the end of February 1941 there were general strikes in Amsterdam and neighboring towns to protest the seizure and deportation of the Jewish population; in April-May 1943 another wave of strikes took place in protest against orders to have former Dutch soldiers reinterned in Germany. Over 150 Dutch were executed on that occasion. In September 1944, in response to airborne landings in Holland, some thirty thousand railwaymen heeded a call from London to strike, despite resulting severe food shortages to the general population.

Underground activities also included the sheltering of Jews, workers about to be transported to Germany for forced labor, members of the armed forces who refused to report for reinternment, and university students who refused to sign declarations of loyalty to Germany. Many of those "underground" lived more or less normal lives with forged papers—by the fall of 1944, it is estimated, some 300,000 people in Holland lived "underground."

There was little large-scale sabotage until late in the war, but raids were conducted on offices to obtain papers, destroy records, and confuse the German deportation system. By the end of the European war, nevertheless, there were some 4,100 men enrolled in the Dutch forces of the interior; they had 1,575 sten guns (dropped by the British); but they would have been faced, in any potential insurrection, by 17,000 German garrison troops.

It was because of these difficult conditions that "the energy which individual Dutchmen wanted to put into the work of the resistance, was poured into channels different from . . . elsewhere. There was much spiritual resistance." [16] That is, civilian defense took place as a last resort, not as a desirable choice.

In Holland, too, appeared a documented case of the occupying army making use of an underground. The Germans, by capturing a handful of underground radio operators and forcing their collaboration, managed for over a year to keep British intelligence convinced that all was well. Forty-nine agents, ninety tons of explosives, eight hundred sten guns, and two thousand hand guns fell into German hands this way, despite the fact that the captive operators followed security procedures and broadcast danger signals. The Germans arrested four hundred other underground workers as a result, and as much as 95 per cent of supplies sent during 1942 and 1943 never reached the underground; the comparative figure for Belgium was 30 per cent, for France 10 per cent. [17]

Pacifist writers have made much of the Danish, Norwegian, and Dutch resistance movements. But it would be a serious error to confuse the use of some non-violent tactics within a broad resistance movement with a "non-violent movement." None of the World War II resistance movements was non-violent. All used some non-violent or a-violent tactics, such as strikes. But the core of every resistance movement, ultimately, was armed resistance, with the end goal of armed insurrection against the Axis occupying power, and with varying degrees of collaboration with the Allied armed forces.

A later consequence of resistance activity, particularly against the Japanese, was that the resistance organizations became the core of future guerrilla wars of liberation against subsequent colonial masters—for example, in Indo-China, the Huks in the Philippines (who are still active), Malaya, and of course the Chinese Communist Revolution itself. The Greek uprising in 1947 also had its origins in World War II. Some of the African liberation movements were at least influenced by military techniques learned in World War II.

The history of underground movements acting by themselves has not been a happy one. As Feliks Gross reminds us, "The Poles had an excellent underground organization throughout history. From the end of the eighteenth century they organized an uprising or a major revolution every thirty years—1794, 1831, 1863, 1904, and 1944 . . . All the insurrections failed." [18]

ARMED DEFENSE

More overt than an underground, yet not revolutionary because it does not intend a seizure of power, is the phenomenon sometimes known as "the self-defense group." It is more revolutionary because it directly confronts the power structure with a visible challenge to normal law enforcement; yet it usually has less ideology, less politics, and ultimately less of a perspective than the underground or resistance movement, which sees itself as a future government. The defense group can, on occasion, escalate into a paragovernment (taking on other functions of government in the absence of a functioning government), and then find itself in an insurrectionary situation it did not intend. This may also happen when the government thinks the defense group is insurrectionary and proceeds to attack and repress it, as in the case of the Black Panthers. As this often results in indiscriminate attacks on innocent members of the general population, inside which the defense group operates, such repression generates allies for the defense group in the same way that counter-terror against terrorists does.

Two recent American examples of defense groups have been the Black Panther party in California and the Deacons for Defense and Justice in as many as fifty Southern communities. The Ku Klux Klan originated after the Civil War as a combination defense and terrorist group; and most Jewish ghettos in Eastern Europe developed defense squads to protect themselves against pogroms. Likewise, trade unionism over a long period of time developed similar groups; the "Molly Maguires," for example, was a combination defense and terror-sabotage group. In the early 1930's the Trotskyist movement in the United States organized "Workers' Defense Squads" to protect its meetings from the attacks of armed Stalinist thugs. Throughout American history, in fact, it has been a tradition for neighbors to protect other neighbors with arms in the face of real or perceived threats from outsiders. Current efforts by white groups to arm themselves in defense against perceived threats from black rioters are another example, although such activities also fulfill certain psychological functions for the participants. But then, psychological aspects are never absent from such efforts, regardless of sponsorship or grievance.

Pacifists have argued from time to time that armed defense only intensifies and escalates hostility between groups. This may be true *at first*. Certainly, antagonistic *attitudes* are often inflamed when an opposing group behaves in a hostile way. Advocates of armed defense, on the other hand, have argued that it deters violence. This is also true, particularly when it comes to *action* rather than attitudes. That is, hostile attitudes may initially increase in response to armed defense while hostile actions simultaneously decrease (out of fear of retaliation). In situations where police are effectively and impartially enforcing laws against violent action, attitudes tend to follow, thus lowering both hostile actions and hostile attitudes. Armed defense appears when police fail to enforce laws effectively and impartially, so that the defense group acts *in loco* the police—it becomes the enforcer of society's super-ego, and if it is effective it can thwart terroristic actions. The potential terrorist, who needs to justify his inability to act under these conditions, later begins to modify his attitudes as well, in the same way he does when the police function.

Armed defense, then, appears only when regular police power has failed, or when such power acts openly on behalf of the opposition. If the police were functioning properly, an armed defense group would be unnecessary. Whether the defenders are socialists or blacks, the basic point is the same: the police are not to be trusted; they are agents of the oppressors, allies of the terrorists who must be defended against. Socialists have held this view since the time of Marx; in one way or another it is a view common among oppressed groups, including, variously, working-class elements (especially in Europe) and peasants, and it is commonly found in the writings of black Americans. The evidence in such sources as the *Reports* of the U.S. Commission on Civil Rights over the years supports such a perception.

A good deal of attention has been focused on armed defense in recent years in connection with the civil rights movement. In 1957, under the leadership of an ex-Marine, Robert F. Williams, some of the members of the Monroe, North Carolina, NAACP obtained a National Rifle Association charter and organized a defense group of some sixty men. Ultimately the group disbanded and Williams fled the country after a kidnaping charge was placed against him; but he claims that during the sit-ins of 1960 "There was less violence in . . . Monroe . . . because we showed willingness to defend ourselves . . . we've had less violence because we've shown the willingness and the readiness to fight . . ." [19] In a study of a Deacons group, another observer noted, "Negroes . . . are aware that it is now much less likely that they will be the victims of arbitrarily administered white violence." And the Deacons group is functional in preventing Negro violence as well: "The Defenders [as the group is called in Harold Nelson's study] was created in the atmosphere of an impending riot. Since its creation, the community has been free from even a rumor of a possible riot." [20] This is so because the defense group acts as a deterrent to white violence that is a contributing factor in causing riots to begin with. Furthermore, the existence of the Deacons does not preclude non-violent action. The Deacons only defend; the non-violent movement acts to change conditions in a more general way, working on issues like discriminatory hiring practices.

The way in which a defense group moves into the political arena can be seen more directly in the case of the Black Panther Party for Defense, now called simply the Black Panther party, a brother party to the white California Peace and Freedom party. It has lobbied, logically enough, against gun-control legislation, on one occasion invading the California legislature with guns in hand. It seems to have been less effective than some Deacon groups in preventing violence, however; a gunfight with Oakland police in April 1968 resulted in one Panther killed, another, the novelist Eldridge Cleaver, wounded, and nine leaders arrested, including Cleaver Another leader and one of the founders, the Panthers' chief military tactician, Huey P. Newton, was already in prison at the time; Newton was, in 1968, a Peace and Freedom party candidate for the United States Congress. On August 5, 1968, a Panther was killed and another fatally wounded by police in Los Angeles.

Two possible reasons why the Panthers have not been successful in inhibiting violence may be, first, that they do not have as much backing from the black community as did the Deacons (perhaps because of their more radical political stance), and, second, that their target is not extra-legal terrorist groups but the police force itself, which is seen as *the* terrorist threat. Armed defense against extra-legal terrorists does not, as such, threaten the police, and may actually function to support the efforts of moderates to create a viable status quo. But armed defense against the police force is a challenge to the status quo and will therefore provoke a more vigorous and repressive policy.

A less direct example of a defense group becoming political is the juvenile gang, a proto-defense group in the sense that it defends a geographic area against intrusions by other gangs, outside the law. But when such fighting gangs "go social," that is, take up welfare and related political activities, their defense function is usually eliminated. With a group like the Panthers, the defense function is consciously seen as being politically revolutionary in perspective, and remains a central focus.

The Minutemen clearly do not fall into the category of armed defense. They and the Klan are, rather, subversive secret societies of a counter-revolutionary sort. They are potential underground or resistance movements, if not outright insurrectionary groups under certain foreseeable circumstances. Their activities include terrorist plots and outright terrorism, and paramilitary activities short of armed attacks, such as drilling and accumulation of arms, including illegal ones. In general they are "in possession of a fairly sophisticated organization, not unlike those of paramilitary units." [21] The Minutemen are counter-revolutionary in the sense that their intent is not to move until a "communist takeover"; but so long as that decision is theirs unilaterally, and the definition is theirs to make and change as they see fit, this assurance is far from comforting.

TRADITIONAL RISINGS

Related to underground and resistance movements are short-lived uprisings in which the population is mainly unarmed, and in which the uprising usually begins with strikes and large-scale street demonstrations. The June 1953 uprising in East Berlin and the June 1956 uprising in Poznan, Poland, are examples. Both were scarcely more than general strikes with attendant marches and rioting, followed by fraternization with troops and some turning over of arms by troops to the people. Revolutions have begun, of course, with less; but in Berlin the Soviet Army moved in quickly to suppress the rising, and in Poznan, in a somewhat different outcome, the Gomulka regime instituted a series of reforms and defused the rising that way. The Hungarian rebellion (October 1956) was more of a national uprising against the USSR, and the Hungarian army aided the rebellion. Even so, Soviet troops and tanks suppressed it within a week or so. It is instructive that the center of the uprising was the city of Budapest, marking this as primarily an urban insurrection (with peasant support); the Soviet regime did not hesitate to lay the city, including some of the most active and militant members of the Hungarian working class, to waste.

The general strike–insurrection was the Marxian model for starting a revolution, and as such had the urban working class as prime mover in mind. The Paris Commune (of which more later), the Petrograd insurrections in February and November 1917, and, historically, the wave of uprisings of 1848, all began this way and formed a basic part of the Marxist revolutionary *corpus* for many years. "Armed revolt," as one leading revolutionist put it, "is the traditional method of revolution, and it is very difficult to deny that hardly any examples of successful revolution by peaceful means are to be found in history." [22]

By the end of the nineteenth century, the general rules of insurrectionary warfare were well understood: arm the workers, disarm the forces of the status quo. Failing either one, the revolt would be crushed. "Blanqui's followers, in 1839, went from gun-shop to gun-shop looting, in order to fulfill the first half of this instruction." [23] Neither they, nor similar attempts in recent American history, were able to accomplish the second; the first is easier.

THE GENERAL STRIKE

A part of the tactic of the general strike is aimed at disarming the forces of the status quo, though on occasion it has been successful even without arming the workers. In March 1920, for example, a German general strike succeeded in foiling an attempted coup by the military without arming the workers.

The general strike, basically a-violent (rather than truly non-violent), is a tactic devised partially to surmount the dangers of armed insurrection, and sometimes can create a revolutionary society even in the course of struggle. Generally defensive, the strike, by totally (or nearly so) immobilizing a community or a nation, can prevent decisions from being carried out. This was the philosophy of the Second (Socialist) International before World War I; its failure to live up to pledges to strike rather than fire upon fellow workers across national borders led to the demise of the International as a revolutionary force, and undermined confidence in the tactic as well.

The general strike is revolutionary only when the strikers go beyond the withholding of work to the seizing of the factories and ultimately of the government—and thus actually continuing to work rather than withholding it. But they must go even further, for "nobody can, from the control of one city . . . proceed to control a whole [national] community and replan it . . . You must go forward to a national capture of power . . ." [24] If a general strike is localized it can be broken because it can be waited out by a power structure, particularly if it is not accompanied by armed insurrection. If it is part of an insurrection, it faces the problems common to all violent outbreaks. Only if it is society-wide, if it seizes rather than stops production, and if it is able to stop the armed forces (as part of the strike) can it succeed. This does not mean that a strike or seizure must be total—key industries suffice (distributive, communications, and some heavy industry in particular). But such a combination of circumstances has not *yet* occurred.

THE ARMED INSURRECTION

An armed insurrection or rebellion may develop "spontaneously" out of a "rising" or series of strikes, or even out of rioting; or it may result from carefully laid plans developed by a conspiratorial group or a well-established resistance movement. In all of these possibilities, the social roots of such action must be kept in mind; that is, no rebellion is truly spontaneous, any more than there is such a thing as spontaneous combustion. The materials for unrest must be present. What looks like spontaneity, therefore, is nothing more than the lighting of the fuse.

The spontaneous rising or general strike may develop into an insurrection, or it may not. The strikes in East Berlin in 1953 and in Poznan in 1956 developed into risings, but not into real rebellions in the sense that an overthrow of the government was seriously attempted. Most general strikes have not even gone as far as a rising. The Seattle general strike of 1919, for example, explicitly disavowed revolutionary political demands and limited itself to traditional trade union demands—only radicals and, conversely, conservatives saw the strike as having revolutionary implications. Both groups were wrong. Street demonstrations involving direct action (in the attempt to dislocate, say, traffic, or troop trains), even when they become involved in some defensive violence (erecting barricades against massive police assaults, hurling objects at police using gas, and so forth), also rarely develop into an actual insurrection.

93 Paramilitary Activities in Urban Areas

The closest thing to insurrectionary outbreak in recent times in a Western setting was the period of combined strike-student demonstrations in France in May and June 1968. In that series of events student demonstrations (including street barricades and Columbia University–type occupations of buildings) with overtly revolutionary designs coincided with French trade-union strikes that developed into virtually a general strike. The society was brought to a standstill by the combined operation, but the revolution was "co-opted" by the political leadership of the leftist parties, including the Communists, which chose to keep political decision-making within the confines of party activity and take it "off the streets." It was as close as any Western urban nation has come to revolution in the last half of the twentieth century. Had the Communist party chosen to abandon parliament and move into the streets (perhaps setting up "revolutionary action committees," as in Czechoslovakia in 1948), a civil war–revolutionary war might have resulted, with all its attendant risks and potentials. The party apparently deemed the risks, which it saw as perhaps including armed intervention by the United States, too great.

It was also apparent that French factory workers were not prepared to go as far as the students; their demands were oriented primarily toward fuller participation in French society rather than an overthrow of it. The students, on the other hand, seemed to be more thoroughly alienated from the system. The parallel with Columbia University and some other situations in which students have been temporarily allied with a black protest movement is striking. In the American case, as in the French, the students played a more radical role, only to have that role undermined by the non-students' (in some cases, black students') acceptance of compromises with immediate material payoffs. This seems to suggest that the system was able to make concessions that made sense to that partner in the "revolution" whose material condition required attention to immediate demands. With the "united front" thus disrupted, the student radicals were unable to come up with positive demands that might have held their allies—or attracted new allies— for further struggle.

This point is particularly interesting in discussing an American revolutionary perspective. While American radical students no longer look to the working class as a potential radical ally (as they once did in the 1930's), they do look to the urban black population (in the same way that they and others look to the peasant in the developing world). The militant rhetoric of the black nationalist tends to support such a perspective, but students do not realize that militant rhetoric is often a cover for relatively moderate demands which do not in any basic way challenge the system, any more than the demands of the French workers for shorter hours with the same pay, or even limited worker-participation in factory decisions, challenged the French system. Black rhetoric sounds radical because it puts moderate demands into a racial (sometimes a separatist) context. But this "radicalism" is perfectly acceptable even to conservative representatives of the system. Revolution predicated on an alliance with forces whose demands *at this point* are still so easily met is foredoomed.

The risks of insurrection are always great; more insurrections have failed than not. Warfare is, after all, conducted like a zero-sum game: the successes of one side are more or less proportional to the defeats of the other. Thus an insurrection, too, succeeds to the degree that the government is unable to contain and defeat it, and the government in turn maintains itself or is toppled depending on the weaknesses and strengths of its antagonists. At the same time, these two forces interact within a wider social and historical context, which largely shapes the characteristics of the antagonists and therefore the outcome.

An insurrection can be successful only if (1) it has achieved the support *or neutrality* of the vast majority of the population; and (2) the dominant power structure is unwilling or unable, for whatever reason, to function in a coordinated manner either to suppress it or to solve the structural strains which give rise to it. The two points are related—the ability of government to suppress revolt or to solve problems is closely related to the support or cooperation of certain functionally essential elements in the population, specifically in the military forces, the economic structure, the political decision-making arena, and, less importantly, among those who offer an ideological rationale for the status quo (in religion, philosophy, the academy, and so forth). As such support diminishes, government fails to function; the more it fails to function, the more support diminishes. The function of terrorism and sabotage in augmenting such conditions has already been discussed. Conversely, if government is able to function, it obtains more support, and so the cycle can be reversed.

Urban paramilitary, guerrilla, or insurrectionary activity by itself, either preceded by a resistance (underground) movement or by more spontaneous events, can be successful in overturning the established order only where that order is already so decayed that a mere push will suffice—Petrograd in 1917, or Caracas in 1958. That is, it will normally be part of a nationwide revolutionary movement, often equal partners with or even subordinate to rural guerrilla activity. In cases where it is not related to rural activity, the countryside will at least have been neutralized, and the communications system which normally would function to bring aid to a beleaguered government will have been disrupted or struck.

No reputable analyst gives any revolution a chance unless the general population has been at least neutralized by the structural strains mentioned earlier. No writer, from conservative to radical, suggests that an urban insurrection can avoid defeat once the rebels are geographically isolated and the government is in a position to move against them in a unified fashion. Recalling the second part of the classical formula—

that the task of an insurrection is to disarm the status quo—
it is clear that modern technology, particularly the speed of
communication and travel, has made that harder than ever to
accomplish, even with a general strike. The use of such devices as helicopters, light bombers, and gas and napalm, while
not excluding revolutionary outbreaks, makes them much
more costly than a century ago. Instructions for looting sporting-goods stores and storming the Pentagon (violently or
otherwise) "are as out of date as manuals on pike-making
and barricade building." [25] As long ago as 1895, in an introduction to Marx's *Class Struggle in France, 1848 to 1850,*
Engels pointed out that street fighting had become obsolete in
1849. "In the future," he reminded revolutionaries, "street
fighting can be victorious only if this disadvantageous situation is compensated by other factors." In the main, he argued,
armed insurrection simply plays into the hands of the ruling
class, giving its military agents an opportunity to destroy
revolutionary forces.

Other observers, ranging from government counter-insurgency experts to Regis Debray, agree with this prognosis.
"The prospects for effective resistance through massive urban
terrorism and sabotage are no more promising [than successful rural operations in high-density, urbanized societies]; a
powerful occupying force, determined to impose its control
and deterred by neither scruples nor military threats from the
outside, can subjugate any city . . . The difficulties groups
may experience in a densely populated area are obvious. The
great number of potential informers, together with police surveillance, identity and ration cards, block wardens, security
checks at work and in the streets . . . handicap the movement
of armed groups," as Peter Paret and John W. Shy bluntly
put it.[26]

No underground, according to Gross, can succeed by itself.
"Without outside support, without an internal crisis . . . social
unrest or international defeat [a resistance movement] does

not succeed . . . Mortal crisis of the . . . system and strong outside political or even military support are essential elements." [27] Debray's description of South American miners holds for urban workers in general: they are "bound to their place of work, together with the women . . . and the children; exposed to all kinds of reprisals . . . without the material possibility of turning themselves into a mobile force [they] are simply condemned to slaughter." [28]

For this reason, in part, Debray condemns urban uprisings. They are provocative; they are targets for repression, as in fact are peasants who aid guerrilla movements. This is why he advocates an elite-led rural-based insurrection. But a rural-based insurrection is possible only in a predominantly rural society in which the peasant is the prime sufferer. In an urban society like the United States, in which there are relatively few peasants, and farmers are almost uniformly hostile to leftist ideas, Debray's approach is ludicrous. The alternative, then, must be to maximize the internal crisis of a society in order to minimize the effectiveness of the armed forces.

The expansion of sabotage and terror activities in the underground-resistance phase is one way of attempting to deal with this problem. Even in urban areas some guerrillas can operate continuously in bands—not, to be sure, in a single community, but possibly in a larger megalopolitan area—for example, the German Ruhr, or perhaps in the area from New Haven south to Baltimore or Washington.[29]

An auxiliary strategy almost always advocated by revolutionists is that of subverting the armed forces and the police by means of propaganda, especially through their families. Such propaganda, Raymond Postgate says, should suggest that the army and police consist of men of high character who are being misused in attacking the unemployed and suppressing black nationalists. Their own grievances must be given attention as well.

Several newspapers devoted to propaganda inside the United

States armed forces demonstrate this basic approach. Here is an excerpt from an article in a paper called *Vietnam GI:* "You got to be off the wall not to see where all this [urban disturbances] is heading. Every year it gets worse. We may end up drafting men to fight—not in the Nam, but in Atlanta, Chicago, New York, and L.A. Are we going to have black and white guys who served together in the Nam killing each other in the States?" [30]

This propaganda strategy is diametrically opposed to the "confrontation" strategy which tries to isolate the police by labeling them "pigs." While such name-calling may have a function, it is not that of trying to reach the opponent and win him over. Rather, as Fanon points out, it can serve to build confidence and morale in an oppressed group. The issue then becomes whether such morale-building cannot be done in ways that will not intensify hostility in armed opponents. Confrontation strategy is not effective in "converting" forces who are convinced they are right; on the contrary, it helps these forces confirm their image of the opposition as a low, vile group worthy only of being smashed by billy-clubs.

Confrontation name-calling, or "shock therapy," can be effective only with opponents who think they are something they are not. Police do not generally suffer from this ailment; moderates do. For example, when a black nationalist calls a policeman a "pig" he may be building up his own morale, but he only confirms the policeman's attitudes about blacks. On the other hand, when he calls a white liberal a "white racist snake," he may force some real introspection in him, possibly leading to some change.

Enemy troops or police rarely "go over" to their opponents. More frequently they become neutral and disappear from the battle area. The general principles outlined by Postgate seem to suggest an effective beginning if such a development is desired.

Although the armed forces' opposition to insurrection can

sometimes be undermined, the fact remains that so long as the state is able and willing to make "careful, judicious use of military organization [under circumstances] when the majority of members of the dominant class have neither lost their sense of mission nor dismissed political formulas traditionally operating in their favor [in short, remaining] committed to their own ideological justifications on the allocation of wealth and power," defeat will be the likely result of insurrection.[31]

When the state is unable or unwilling to act, the insurrection can become a revolution and win. For example, it is apparent in reading news items from Saigon that urban warfare by guerrillas against regular troops is not impossible, and can indeed make inroads over a long period of time. This seems to be the case where the urban guerrilla forces are regularly supplied from the countryside and are militarily supported from the suburbs and nearby countryside by mobile rocket units and the like. "If you have a determined minority that wants to engage in terrorism, I'm not sure that anyone can stop it," one observer is quoted as saying. "You can infiltrate any city in the world, and in a city this size it can't be prevented."[32] So long as there is somewhere to infiltrate from, so long as the city is not militarily or socially isolated, urban insurrection even in a modern setting is possible. In Quebec Province, Canada, for example, the Front de Liberation de Quebec (FLQ) has rejected rural guerrilla warfare because of the population concentration in Montreal, and because of unfavorable weather conditions. But the Ottawa government cannot seal off and isolate Montreal from the countryside; to do so would provoke large-scale popular support for the FLQ, even among conservative nationalists in rural areas, and thus would create even more favorable conditions for guerrilla warfare. Because of the neutrality and potential support of Quebec farmers, the FLQ is in a far more favorable position than, say, black nationalists in the United States.[33]

Several longer-range conclusions can also be pointed to. The dominant power structure can cope with urban paramilitary activity in two ways, similar in most respects to its strategy in any insurgency war. It can move radically to solve the problems of the population, thus cutting off the guerrilla's base of support in the populace; or it can move to suppress military activity through counter-insurgency warfare and other military means, including aerial bombardment. This seems far more typical.

The "liberal" solution, that of attempting to combine these two strategies, is inherently inconsistent because the use of military means is almost inevitably bound (in an urban situation particularly) to injure the innocent, and, if the guerrillas really come from the local population, win them more support and thereby undermine "the other war," that of reform measures. In addition, the "two-war" strategy is often dangerous because it elicits counter-revolutionary measures from the ultra right, which is threatened by the reforms. The "liberal" way of coping with insurgency is similar in many ways to the "moderate" road to reform in the underdeveloped nation. The liberal or moderate is always caught on the horns of a power dilemma: If he does not promote enough reforms to deal with the society's problems realistically, the left-insurgents will gain strength, sometimes making it more difficult to institute reforms because the social structure is increasingly undermined. If, on the other hand, the reforms are meaningful and the left is undermined, there is always the danger from the right—or the C.I.A. Meaningful reforms threaten the status quo so much that it often sees a counter-revolutionary coup as preferable—leading, if successful, to further growth of the left-insurgents, for their problems remain unsolved.

In short, the "liberal" solution, even where "the other war" side of the "two-war" strategy becomes ascendant, runs the real risk of being undermined if not overthrown from within the Establishment, particularly when the social structure is weak and certain elements in the Establishment feel themselves unusually threatened. This is always the case (almost by definition) once an insurgency war has broken out.

Very often the "two-war" strategy is not really a strategy at all, but rather marks a stage when the power structure has not yet decided how to deal with insurrectionary activity (or urban riots, or demonstrations, and so forth). The appearance of inconsistency which accompanies a "two-war" strategy is an indication of early indecisiveness. But this indecisiveness is perceived as an *inherent* incapacity of the power structure to deal with the situation, hence creating an illusion (for example, among some black revolutionists) that the revolution can win.

It is difficult, sometimes, to judge whether inconsistency is "liberal"—that is, marks a stage when the power structure has *not yet* decided how to deal with insurrection—or whether it marks a stage following the *failure* of the consensus decision (usually a decision to be repressive), hence *truly* indicates inherent weakness. My own view is that the American population by and large has not been neutralized by structural strain, nor is it likely to be sufficiently disaffected within the next decade so as to refuse to support the government in suppressing urban uprisings. All evidence is to the contrary. We are, therefore, still in the pre-consensus stage, and we should have no illusions that the power structure can no longer deal with the problems of our society, perhaps in a repressive manner.

CHAPTER FIVE

THE BLACK GUERRILLA

What are the real prospects for guerrilla warfare in the urban black ghetto? A 1967 Harlem handbill states, "There is but one way to end this suffering and that is by Black Revolution. Our Revolution is a unity of the Black Man wherever he may be . . . When we unite we can end our suffering. Don't riot, join the revolution!" I. F. Stone, on August 19, 1968, commented: "We must be prepared to see first of all that we face a black revolt; secondly, that the black ghettos regard the white police as an occupying army; thirdly, that guerrilla war against this army has begun . . . The effect of the ambushes which have begun to occur in various cities is to deepen police hatred . . . and therefore to stimulate those very excesses and brutalities which have made the police a hated enemy." [1]

On the other extreme, as it were, are warnings emanating from police and army circles. The *New Republic* (January 27, 1968) quotes a Colonel Robert B. Rigg, writing in the January 1968 *Army* magazine, as predicting "scenes of destruction approaching those of Stalingrad in World War II." Colonel Rigg's viewpoint seems to be that ". . . in the next decade at least one major metropolitan area could be faced with guerrilla warfare requiring sizable United States army elements . . ."

If we assume there will in fact be further disorders in our urban ghettos in the years to come, given the general failure of society to solve the problems of the poor and of the black community, and that some of these disorders may well take the form of paramilitary outbursts, what is the prognosis for such insurrectionary attempts?

I assume first of all that a black rebellion would be a genuinely popular uprising and might be able to take over militarily the black ghetto areas of some cities. But if this were to take place, it would be without any logistical base in the countryside or abroad, and the urban uprisings would be territorially and logistically isolated. A further assumption is that of the Black Power advocates themselves, namely, that we live in a basically racist society which would not hesitate to counter with a reactionary, completely military solution to black paramilitary activity. There is ample evidence to support the idea that even racially and culturally similar groups do not balk at such measures. If a serious insurrection were to take place, there is little doubt (at least in my mind) that this would unleash the barely latent hostilities of a large sector of white society, which would support repressive measures. In addition to being isolated in the cities, the black guerrilla would confront a government more or less in a position to move in a unified fashion against him. In brief, the black

guerrilla is in as bad a position as some of the worst examples
of revolt in history (for example, the Warsaw Ghetto) and
is certainly in no way analogous to the more optimal situations (Caracas in 1958, or Petrograd in 1917).

The latter were offensive (revolutionary) in the sense that
the existing government was to be replaced; a black rebellion
would in all likelihood be, like the Warsaw Ghetto uprising,
defensive, meaning that it would be a reaction to further encroachments on the ghetto population by the status quo—
hence an insurrection of desperation. (An alternative strategy,
that of the "inter-urban guerrilla," will be explored later.)

A brief examination of some cases that roughly approxi-
mate the situation of the defensive black guerrilla in the
United States will show, I think, that unless the social structure becomes far weaker than we have reason to believe it
will in the near future, a defensive black insurrection is
doomed from a military point of view.

Some information was gathered covering six cases of urban
uprisings, all but one in this century. Excluded from these
cases were such short-lived risings as those in Berlin and
Poznan in June 1953 and June 1956, respectively; also excluded were general rebellions of which the urban uprising
was only one part—for example, the Hungarian rebellion of
1956 or the Irish Revolution of 1919—and urban uprisings
such as Petrograd and Caracas, where the rebels were neither
isolated nor confronted with a unified power structure.

The following criteria were used in this selection, which, it
should be emphasized, is illustrative rather than a sampling.
First, each uprising was at minimum a guerrilla outbreak,
backed by a significant sector of the local urban population—
that is, each was a genuinely popular "rising." Second, in each
case the rising developed into a rebellion which successfully
took over an entire city or a large sector thereof. Third, the
rebels in each case were isolated, either acting totally alone,
or effectively separated from outside support. Fourth, in these

illustrations the government continued to function effectively at least outside the city, and managed to move in a unified fashion against the rebels within a short time. These are, in fact, the conditions confronting Black Power strategists when they talk about paramilitary activity of an insurrectionary kind.

CASE	DATES	CASUALTIES
The Paris Commune	March 28–May 28, 1871	20,000 to 30,000 dead vs. 83 officers and 794 men of the Versaillese government
The Easter Rising (Dublin)	April 24–29, 1916	No figures available
Shanghai, China	February 21–April 13, 1927	About 5,000 dead
Vienna, Austria	February 12–17, 1934	1,500 to 2,000 dead vs. 102 Heimwehr
Warsaw Ghetto	April 19–May 15, 1943	Several thousand killed, 56,000 deported, vs. about 20 Germans
Warsaw Uprising	July 31–October 2, 1944	100,000 to 250,000 dead

1. *The Paris Commune, March 28–May 28, 1871.* After the capitulation of Paris to the Prussians on January 8, 1871, the Prussian troops remained on the outskirts of the city, preferring to let the conservative Thiers government disarm the more popularly based National Guard which was mainly working class in composition. When the government attempted to do so on March 18, the National Guard resisted, and on the 28th the Commune was proclaimed. The official government withdrew to Versailles, and together with the Prussians besieged the city. The Commune held fast for two months but was finally overwhelmed by the troops of Versailles, with the Prussians playing a relatively passive role. A brutal massacre followed; Frank Jellinek has pointed out that the whole

Jacobin "terror" during the French Revolution executed 2,596 people in Paris; in the Commune between 20,000 and 30,000 men, women, and children fell. How many of these were victims of the massacre is unknown. Over 30,000 people were subsequently imprisoned. The Versaillese forces lost 83 officers and 794 men killed.[2]

2. *The Easter Rising, Dublin, April 24–29, 1916.* Intense repression of Irish nationalism from 1914 to 1916 had built up considerable resentment in the population, and by the fall of 1915 the Irish Volunteers, military arm of the Irish Republican Brotherhood, were drilling and marching openly in many parts of the country, including Dublin. An uprising was fixed for Easter Sunday 1916, but was countermanded at the last minute by the national organization, led by moderates. The Dublin organization, James Connolly's working-class-oriented Citizens' Army, determined to go ahead anyway, and the rebellion broke out on Monday, April 24 with the swift seizure of the Post Office and other key points, and the proclamation of the Republic. Some one thousand to fifteen hundred armed men and women participated. British troops were rushed to the city from thoughout the country, and they gradually forced their way into insurgent areas, backed by artillery fire and raiding parties which took heavy casualties among civilian non-combatants. On Saturday, April 29, the surviving Citizens' Army soldiers surrendered. Connolly himself was severely wounded. Courts-martial quickly followed, and from May 3 to 12, fifteen of the ringleaders, including Connolly, were executed. In 1919 the armed struggle was renewed on a nationwide basis, resulting two years later in an ambiguous treaty with the British. This was followed by a civil war which lasted two more years. Precise casualty figures on the Easter rising are not available.

3. *Shanghai, February 21–April 13, 1927.* In response to Chiang Kai-shek's military advance from the north with a

revolutionary army, the workers of Shanghai staged a general strike on February 19, 1927, to undermine the local warlord and aid Chiang. In response, execution squads were set up on the streets, and after this terror an insurrection began on February 21. Chiang, who was basically hostile to the working-class forces, waited on the outskirts of the city, and the insurrection was suppressed two days later. While Chiang continued to engage himself in mopping-up operations outside the city, the workers again struck on March 21. Again Chiang did not move. This strike also led to an insurrection which succeeded in taking over the city, and Chiang was welcomed as a liberator. But on April 12 Chiang, aided by foreign troops and gangsters, began a reign of terror against working-class, trade union, and communist organizations. After sporadic resistance, the revolutionists were wiped out by Chiang's forces within twenty-four hours. O. Edmund Clubb estimates that about five thousand radicals, unionists, and the like were massacred.[3]

4. *Vienna, February 12–17, 1934.* The Austrian Socialist party had been desperately trying to work out a common front against the Nazis with the Dollfuss regime, despite the latter's physical attacks on the socialists in various parts of the country. The Viennese socialists, representing the city's working class in the main, finally agreed to rise in arms if the Dollfuss government attempted further suppression of workers' organizations in the city. On February 12 the Heimwehr, Dollfuss' military arm, raided Viennese workers' clubs and arrested many leading socialist figures. Armed resistance began when Dollfuss invaded, interestingly, the worker-controlled public housing projects, and fired on the projects with howitzers and mortars. After three days of heavy fighting the survivors were forced to surrender or were overpowered, with some leaders fleeing the country. Nine leaders of the defensive "insurrection" were immediately hanged, and thousands were im-

prisoned in concentration camps. Some fifteen hundred to two thousand people had been killed, as against 102 soldiers of the Heimwehr.

5. *The Warsaw Ghetto, April 19–May 15, 1943*. In the fall of 1942, after only seventy thousand of an original population of 400,000 remained in the Jewish ghetto of Warsaw, the Jewish organizations decided to resist further deportations militarily. The ghetto was more or less in Jewish hands to begin with, and when Weapons-SS raiding parties entered to liquidate the population on the 19th, they were met with gunfire. Only some fifteen hundred Jews were organized into military units, with less equipment among them than in a company of infantry (about a hundred rifles, a few machine guns, a few hundred revolvers). SS and police units numbered two to three thousand. Several thousand Jews were killed in the fighting, some five to six thousand escaped into the surrounding countryside (many to be captured and killed later), and 56,000 were deported to extermination camps. When the Russians arrived in January 1945, only two hundred Jews remained alive in the city.

An interesting historical note for those who believe that in some sense ghetto home rule (including self-policing) is desirable, is that the Warsaw Ghetto was, from 1940 to 1943, virtually a Jewish state. "Yiddish-speaking policemen were a direct consequence of the German decision to establish a ghetto, and in that respect they became as necessary as any other group . . ." [4] This self-rule, wherever it existed among Jews, actually contributed to their destruction by creating a mechanism which the Nazis could and did use to do their work. A similar example occurs in the story of *The Bridge on the River Kwai*, when the discipline and morale infused by a British officer are used by the Japanese to help their military efforts in destroying other British units.

A ghetto is particularly vulnerable to hunger and disease, especially when enforced by a besieging army (as in Warsaw or the Paris Commune). In Paris the people ate rats and shoelaces; in Warsaw hunger and typhus resulted in five thousand deaths each month in the year prior to the ghetto uprising. "By decreasing and choking off the food supply, the Germans were able to turn the ghettos into death traps. And that is what they did." [5] Raul Hilberg reports that in the winter of 1941–42 the sewage pipes froze, toilets became useless, and human excrement was dumped into the streets with the garbage. Cases of cannibalism were reported. Between 500,000 and 600,000 Jews died in Polish ghettos and labor camps *before* the extermination camps went into operation.

6. *The Warsaw Uprising, July 31–October 2, 1944.* As Russian troops approached Warsaw, an underground army, with agreement of the Soviets, rose up to throw out the Germans and divert German troops from the Russian flanks. Preparations were relatively open, as the Germans ignored violations of many regulations. There was a virtual vacuum of power in the city, and the underground was able to take over large sectors of it very quickly. The Russians, however, did not come to the aid of the uprising for political reasons, and the German occupying troops were soon able to make serious inroads into the city. Despite several extremely risky British and American air drops of supplies (and ultimately even Russian ones, though they neglected parachutes so that all supplies were destroyed as they hit the ground), the underground was forced to surrender. The Germans had deported some 200,000 hostages to nearby concentration camps by this time; estimates of total Warsaw casualties for the two-month battle range from 100,000 to 250,000 killed.

Note that in most of these cases the rebels had no illusions about winning without outside aid. In three of the cases (the Easter Rising, Shanghai, and the Warsaw Uprising) the rebels moved on the false assumption that aid would be forthcoming, and in two others they moved only in desperation, with no real hope of success. Even the Paris Commune hoped that the remainder of the country would organize communes to come to its aid. Furthermore, in five of the six cases, the actual outbreak of the rebellion took place only as a defensive measure against severe encroachments by the dominant power, and would probably not have occurred at all without this repression. The Warsaw Uprising is the only exception to this. And, in three of the cases, the rebellion was against foreigners. Perhaps it can be argued that the American white power structure is basically foreign to the black population, but having a clearly foreign oppressor does seem to make it easier to unite the population for rebellion.

Given this sort of dismal evidence, why has so much attention been given by the white press, and by some spokesmen in Black Power circles, to paramilitary potentials? There are three possible interpretations for this fascination (apart from the view that the police and the military display alarm in order to justify their existence and their appropriations). First, paramilitary affairs in the black ghetto may be largely a creation of the press which has resulted in a self-fulfilling prophecy. For the white community, which seems to require a rationale for abandoning the civil rights movement and refusing significant aid to urban areas, the urban riot has become highly functional. The attention given by the white press to what has been until recently the peripheral phenomenon of paramilitary Black Power is equally if not more functional. For lower middle-class people in the suburbs who have long-repressed itchy trigger fingers, talk of urban risings by the black population affords an outlet for repressed hostilities which can only be exceeded by an actual outbreak of warfare. For the black community, the large-scale attention focused upon a small minority of paramilitary types seems evidence that such activity may in fact be dangerous, hence effective as a threat with which to coerce white power structures. Such a view is useful for paramilitary recruiters.

A second, related interpretation has already been discussed in the preceding chapter, in the context of the psychological drawing-power of all violent, action-oriented movements. It has to do with the "machismo" so important to downtrodden males in any oppressed culture.

A third interpretation, which is by now a cliché in social science as well as informed lay circles, has to do with the desperation born of the apparent failure of both conventional politics and non-violent direct action to secure significant changes in the condition of the American Negro. As a result, many black leaders have been forced to the conclusion that, for the time being at least, the civil rights movement is dead and that Black Power—the cultural, social, and economic autonomy (and, given the ghettoized character of the black population, territorial autonomy) of blacks—is the only viable strategy. Black Power is a vague concept because it is a new movement. It should not be surprising that some of its advocates demand violent or military tactics. We must remember that it took from about 1825 to the publication, in 1896, of Herzl's *The Jewish State* for Jews even to begin to clarify the issue of "Jewish Power," and that, almost from the beginnings of Zionism, many Zionist as well as non-Zionist ghetto groups had paramilitary auxiliaries.

A SCENARIO

Despite the pessimistic military prognosis for a black revolution, it "might be attempted in the face of overwhelming odds and without regard to the terrible consequences." [6] Let us see, by the use of a crude scenario, how a defensive black insurrection, born of desperation, might develop. Obviously, any knowledgeable person could add all sorts of complications and refinements to such a scenario by including various technological considerations. Nevertheless, I believe the basic issues can be clearly made to appear in such a semi-fictional presentation.

*

It was a hot Friday evening in August 1969, in the north Philadelphia ghetto. In the third incident in as many weeks, police halted a car belonging to members of the "Black Liberation Front," and, when one of the blacks was slow to get out of the car, police opened fire. Two of the car's occupants were hit; a third returned the fire with an automatic carbine, and an officer was hit. An "assist officer" call went out and soon a several-block area was surrounded by "red cars." Meanwhile, the surviving B.L.F. fighter disappeared. The appearance of the police cars drew catcalls from the young people of the area, and when police attempted to place two youngsters under arrest, a minor riot broke out. Other B.L.F. members had by then been alerted, and within a half-hour a small mob was moving onto the precinct station.

Meanwhile, a half-dozen "triads" of B.L.F. irregulars opened fire on traffic patrolmen and police cars at as many locations in north and west Philadelphia, and other units of less than a dozen men each began to smash store windows along Columbia and Ridge Avenues, the principal ghetto merchant centers. An outraged mob of blacks, at a B.L.F. street-corner rally at 52nd and Market Streets, occupied the train station there and took over the control point of the suburban trains. A trained B.L.F. technician halted the Paoli (suburban) Local.

Almost simultaneously, "Radio Black Liberation" went on the air to declare martial law in north and west Philadelphia, and to announce the formation of a revolutionary government for the defense of the area against further atrocities by the white police "pigs." Control points were established, and whites attempting to enter the area by car or bus were fired on and turned back. "Radio Black Liberation" announced the capture of over one thousand white businessmen and professionals from the Paoli Local. The North Philadelphia Station of the Pennsylvania Railroad was captured after an exchange of gunfire with railway police, and train service to New York City was cut. Irregular B.L.F. units intercepted underground telephone and electricity conduits, and all electricity in Philadelphia, plus a ten-county area in southeastern Pennsylvania and southern New Jersey, was cut off. City Hall, some fifteen blocks from the rebel-held area, was attacked by terrorist groups, and an explosion rocked the police station at 8th and Race, a similar distance from the north Philadelphia ghetto. The police communications system was knocked out, and there were heavy police casualties. North and west Philadelphia, with a total black population of about 400,000 (and less than 100,000 whites), was effectively under rebel control.

B.L.F. activities had been under surveillance for some time. Months before, the Philadelphia Police Commissioner had developed contingency plans in case of a serious uprising, in careful collaboration with state and federal officials. Hints of black unrest had appeared in the local press, and the usual electronic devices, though unconstitutional, kept interested parties informed of most B.L.F. activities. Gun sales in the suburbs and white areas adjacent to the ghetto rocketed; when the Paoli Local was stopped, a few white businessmen even took revolvers and carbines from their attaché cases and managed to scare the rebels off the train station platforms. Thus, while the train remained an isolated hostage in a hostile ghetto, it remained "free." The passengers went hungry that night and the succeeding day; a handful of black passengers was executed.

National Guard units, "trained up" to urban guerrilla warfare duty, and virtually all white, were moved in quickly to confront the rebel control points all along the borders between north and west Philadelphia and the rest of the city. Police cut off the city water supply to the ghetto area, and auxiliary electricity and telephone systems restored service to the remainder of the city and outlying counties. Special Forces units moved by boat to the bridges of the Schuylkill River and cut off communications between north and west Philadelphia. Helicopters began twenty-four-hour surveillance of the rebel areas—the rebels managed to shoot down several of them. By 4 A.M. Saturday morning the rebel area, cut in half, lay in total darkness, surrounded by a division of the Pennsylvania National Guard. "Radio Black Liberation" was effectively forced off the air as its generators carried it only to a fifty-block area. No food supplies of any kind were delivered to the ghetto area Saturday. The Paoli Local, isolated but free, was soon reinforced by pinpoint parachutists of the 110th Airborne, who shot their way out of the station to "liberate" a block area on each side. Helicopters using flame-throwers prepared the way; extensive fires soon raged in west Philadelphia—there was of course no fire service, and no water.

By noon Saturday, dissension in rebel ranks began to build as deputations of neighbors pleaded for surrender. There was no milk, no bread, no water; the sewage system was hopelessly backed up, and the almost negligible medical personnel left in the area warned of imminent epidemics. Looting of stores was complete, but the food supplies could not last long. Outbreaks in other Northern cities, which the B.L.F. had hoped for, either failed to materialize or were similarly isolated. In any case, the rebels received no accurate information from the outside, and they could not even know of the protests entered on their behalf by several African nations. (The Soviet Union remained silent, having just suffered a reprimand from the United Nations General Assembly for its intervention in the internal affairs of Rumania.)

At 2 P.M. on Saturday, deputations of National Guard officers, including Negro officers, made appearances in both west and north Philadelphia. Upon being taken to rebel headquarters, they stated that unless the rebels surrendered unconditionally by 5 P.M., artillery units would proceed to demolish north Philadelphia block by block. The rebel command repeated the famous utterance made by the United States commander at Bastogne, in World War II, adding, "What the hell, it's cheaper than urban renewal."

Meanwhile, however, two other events in the city came to light in the press (which appeared that day as usual, with appeals for law and order which were dropped into the ghetto area). First, south Philadelphia, the location of Philadelphia's third black community, was placed under martial law—a pass system was instituted, and several hundred potential "troublemakers" were quickly arrested and shipped to a neighboring county jail, which had been taken over by a National Guard battalion. Second, at the border of north Philadelphia and neighboring Kensington, National Guard units were alternated with units of the Kensington Citizens' Militia, which, unlike the National Guard, began a tactic of quick hit-and-run invasions of the rebel-controlled area. Several dozen blacks were killed in these raids, which demolished, by explosive, several tenements. Eleven militiamen fell casualty to the rebels. By 3 P.M. Saturday, eight blocks were evacuated and left in the hands of the Kensington Militia, while no blocks were gained anywhere against the National Guard and the Airborne troops.

Promptly at 5 P.M. a field artillery battalion of the 1st Army, headquartered at Fort Dix, entrenched itself in a schoolyard ten blocks below the ghetto area and proceeded to level the area bordered by Broad, Columbia, 15th and Jefferson Streets, in the heart of north Philadelphia. A half-hour later an Air Force jet dropped napalm on the Muslim Mosque on Lancaster Avenue in west Philadelphia, starting an uncontrollable fire.

Events after that time were indistinct. It would seem that a crowd of black women, some armed, overran the rebel post at Presbyterian Hospital in west Philadelphia and surrendered to the National Guard. Except for one public housing project, in which snipers continued activity until Sunday morning, west Philadelphia was occupied by midnight. North Philadelphia held out longer because of fear of the Kensington Militia, but word of this finally leaked out through the City's Human Relations Commission, and the Militia was withdrawn; a committee of Negro ministers surrendered the area to the Guard in a brief, prayerful ceremony at noon Sunday. The "Philadelphia Commune" was over, less than forty-eight hours after it began.

More than two thousand "rebels," most of them women and children, perished, as against some one hundred Guardsmen (mostly victims of sniper fire), some dozen Airborne and two dozen civilians (in the battle of the Paoli Local), eleven Kensington Militiamen, and twenty police officers.

*

This sort of outcome has been the common fate of isolated urban uprisings. Coordinated uprisings in many cities would complicate matters, of course; so would supporting paramilitary actions (including, perhaps, seizures of public buildings and even police stations) by left-wing students. But so long as the general public (including about 800,000 members of the National Rifle Association) is prepared to support the government, even a larger-scale uprising can have hardly any other result.

There is a possible exception; if, in a pre-consensus "liberal" stage the government acts inconclusively, the rebellion might last longer. But, again given the prognosis of general public hostility to the aims of the rebels, pressure on the government from the right would probably be so extreme that a military solution might be forced. If the government continued to vacillate, a threatened right-wing coup (or, at minimum, right-wing vigilante action) would force the government to "clean up the mess" rather than be forced from office.

Let us suppose, however, that the Philadelphia Commune had been able to hold out for a few more days, and that the government had proposed a negotiated settlement. What might the rebels have demanded? It is difficult to say, particularly since the black community is itself divided on broad strategy. But one might suppose the following kinds of demands: (1) Self-government with the election of a black mayor and council in the black-held area. (2) Expropriation of all white-owned businesses, with ownership passing to the community (socialization). (3) Black autonomy over all institutions in the rebel area, including public schools, welfare institutions, and housing. (4) Political recognition as a separate city-state, or perhaps in cooperation with other such communes, as a nation, with diplomatic representation. (5) Free passage to and from work in white areas, with economic relationships roughly approximating those of the "common market," i.e., a common monetary standard, trade agreements, no tariffs, and so on.

Such an arrangement is not dangerous to white society in any fundamental way, and in fact it is one of the Establishment strategies briefly summarized in the Introduction to this book. Demographically, black government is in the cards for many American cities anyway, so long as city-county consolidation (the abolition of artificial city boundaries) is resisted by the suburbs. With the exception of the landlord and small-merchant class (and a few larger distributors like those of dairy products, who would have to give way to black cooperatives), the advantages to the economy would probably outweigh the disadvantages. White society might still be able to hire black mercenaries to fight its colonial wars. And a wasteful welfare establishment could be dismantled in much the same way as with a guaranteed minimum income, except that the black community alone would have to generate that income rather than the whole nation.

In the short run, most of the economic disadvantages of the plan would be to the black community. Many more would be unemployed before whites caught on to the advantages (and basically harmless nature) of the black-controlled internal neo-colony. It would take some years before enough capital could be generated inside the black community to reach the "take-off" point of economic development, and black businesses (whether privately controlled or socially owned and controlled) would then have to confront the problem of competition with white businesses which would probably be discriminatory. This new discrimination could only be overcome by competing economically, which would in all probability mean cutting labor costs and installing labor-saving machinery. The black community would then have an unemployment rate roughly similar to its rate at present, but at a higher level of expectation. In terms of *general* economic conditions it would continue to be dependent on the white economy because of its need to trade with the outside world.

Trotsky once said you cannot have socialism in one country. Nor can you have it, isolated, in one ghetto or even in a set of ghettos. The economic future of the black American is, for better or worse, tied to a national and, in fact, an international economy. Separate economies are no longer viable even if they were not prevented by the dominant social order for racist reasons. (One can imagine how racists would use the fact that blacks were economically and politically no longer a part of the United States.)

Black Power circles have mentioned an alternative form of paramilitary activity in the urban context—the longer-range revolutionary underground, possibly including terrorism, sabotage, and even small, mobile guerrilla bands, all of this being carried on over a longer period of years. The objective of such a strategy would be similar to that of Debray in Latin America: to create such social havoc that the structure of society would be subverted. With such subversion, and the inability of the regime to cope with the problems created by it, other elements of society would also become disaffected, and the guerrilla movement would in this way gradually grow to a point where an attempt to overthrow the entire government might be made. Ths strategy would assume some allies among whites.

Such a prognosis makes more sense. "The new concept is lightning campaigns conducted in highly sensitive urban communities with the paralysis reaching the small communities and spreading to the farm areas. . . . It dislocates the organs of harmony and order and reduces central power to the level of a helpless, sprawling, octopus . . . The factory workers will be afraid to venture out on the streets to report to their jobs. . . . Violence and terror will spread like a firestorm. A clash will occur inside the armed forces . . . U.S. forces will be spread too thin for effective action . . . The economy will fall into a state of chaos." [7]

The obstacles to this strategy, unlike that of the insurrectionary outbreak as such, are not as serious as the House Committee on Un-American Activities might think—it is questionable that "there is little doubt that such an uprising could be effectively and quickly controlled." It is not true, either, that "the ghetto could be isolated and the guerrillas effectively bottled up," unless all ghettos were turned into concentration camps—which would create precisely the conditions for immediate, widespread insurrection that some militants might like. Nor is it true that "a guerrilla war based on racial lines would never be supported by any sizable number of Negroes . . .," especially if the Committee's suggestion that the ghetto should be isolated and "search and seizure operations . . . instituted" is followed. [8]

What HCUA has done is to support the idea that an actual

outbreak of insurrection at present would be suicidal. But it has not effectively demolished the arguments for a gradual buildup, beginning with terrorism and sabotage on a small scale. Indeed, it supports such a strategy by pointing (accurately, I think) to the way our government would react once such a campaign were begun: "most civil liberties would have to be suspended . . . the population of the ghetto would be classified through an office for the 'control and organization of the inhabitants.' . . ." We might even see the institution of puppet governments, and puppet police, and, of course, "The McCarran Act provides for various detention centers . . ." This, then, is the sure road to the subversion of the country, and to a revolution—or a counter-revolution. Who will have been chiefly responsible, the rebels or the police state created to control them?

THE INTER-URBAN GUERRILLA

Let us look at a scenario of an inter-urban guerrilla campaign, devised as a strategy to subvert society and create a revolutionary situation.

*

By 1972 the Black Liberation Front had established small followings in virtually every black ghetto from Boston to Washington, D.C., including elements numerically strong enough to form small guerrilla bands in most larger cities of that megalopolis. The strategy of the B.L.F. followed traditional resistance or revolutionary underground lines: small triads consisting of one "leader," one "agit-prop" (agitation and propaganda), and one "org-man" (organizational work) were in touch with district triads through only one man (to reduce the risk of informers); each district was in contact with an area triad, each area with a region, and so forth, all the way up to the top. The capture of any member would involve, at most, the other members of his triad, and by that time security procedures would warn others to change location, names, and identity papers. Each triad, in addition, had special functions: supply, intelligence, assault, training, or "underground railway" for smuggling people in and out of Mexico, Canada, and other points farther away (Cuba, for example). Assault units often were smuggled to Canada, trained in sabotage and terror methods (in Quebec province), and then returned. Other training areas included isolated farms in Pennsylvania, the Adirondacks, and the Catskills.

Only assault units were fully armed; other units had some arms, but their operations did not require extensive violence, thus minimizing legal risks. The assault teams as well as other units were required to manufacture most of their own sabotage equipment; supply units functioned only to obtain special equipment such as radios, trucks, machine guns, and larger stores of explosives. "Normal" arms were purchased in small quantities over the counter or occasionally looted from sporting-goods stores, or seized from "the man on the beat" (who was gradually replaced throughout the country by mobile police units).

The main operating areas for the B.L.F. guerrilla bands were the larger cities, especially its police and government operations, with some attention to nearby army and naval bases; later, industrial sites were targeted. The objective was to "get whitey out" by dislocating his system. Two methods of operation were used chiefly: night attacks using a large ghetto as a base, then returning singly to that base to merge with the population (including holding down a regular job). Police found it difficult to track single fighters back into enemy "jungle." The second method was to base small bands in nearby cities, move them to a point of attack, and then out of that area to other nearby cities (usually smaller, less significant, and more neglected by enforcement officials). For example, in the attack on West Point of Christmas Day 1972, ten triads converged from as many small cities, and dispersed to as many others. To this day, enforcement officials do not know who came from what city, or who went where—all that is known is that at least Poughkeepsie, Beacon, Newburgh, Nyack, Ossining, Peekskill, and White Plains were involved. Each had a black ghetto; each had proto-political "disturbances" in the late sixties, and none had its problems significantly dealt with, much less solved, by 1972.

Between 1970 and 1973, ambushes of law enforcement agents increased rapidly; by 1972 one-man police cars were no longer used in the megalopolis. Even state police traveled in pairs on highway and turnpike patrol duty. Nevertheless, an average of five police teams were attacked every week during the last six months of 1972.

By early 1973 the B.L.F. felt itself strong enough to expand operations. In April of that year eight police stations, two National Guard armories, three city jails, and a minimum-security federal prison were raided. All weapons were taken, and all prisoners released from jails. Martial law had to be declared in four cities, and one division of army troops was recalled from Germany. The President was unable to promise the military dictator of Thailand further military aid—the President's inauguration, significantly, had had to be moved from Washington, as his nomination was moved from San Francisco the summer before, in response to general strikes by the black populations in those cities.

Sabotage of industrial production began that spring. Behind the scenes, industrial leaders demanded action to halt the rapidly mounting economic chaos, and military men called the President's attention to the fact that most military stockades were now overflowing with black soldiers and their white "peacenik" friends. The naval facility at Newport News was heavily damaged by sabotage, which coincided with riots in two state prisons (allegedly instigated by Muslims) and a

Marine Corps brig. The assassination of the Governor of Virginia further served to undermine law and order. Several banks were "hit" for funds to carry out B.L.F. actions.

The national response to this situation was mixed. On the left, liberals and radicals called for full implementation of the "political program" of the B.L.F., which demanded a pullout of white power from black ghettos, and the socialization of the ghettos. In addition, realizing the limits of the ghetto economy, white radicals demanded the nationalization of basic industries and their full assistance to the black economy without strings attached.

In the political center, such groups as Americans for Democratic Action and the Urban Coalition, as well as many trade unions, demanded a "war on two fronts," the establishment of law and order, and social measures to alleviate the ghetto's problems. These programs included a guaranteed income, local control over urban renewal, decentralization of education and welfare, with control to be handed over to local citizen groups, an extensive "Freedom Budget," and better-trained and better-paid police. The *Wall Street Journal* considered this a "realistic" program.

On the right, vigilante and "neighborhood defense" groups sprang up by the hundreds. The National Rifle Association and the American Legion merged to form the largest paramilitary organization in world history. On the ultra-right, the Minutemen flourished.

Crisis after crisis virtually immobilized organized religion and the multiversity. It was no longer possible to recruit theology students to serve local (especially surburban) churches and synagogues. The universities were riddled with unrest and demands for student and faculty power. Almost every professional organization in the country, from social workers and sociologists to physicists and political scientists, had "left" caucuses which demanded an end to "serving the establishment" and a reorientation of professions and the universities to "human needs," which they often saw as revolution. The universities became training centers for direct action and non-violent resistance. There was a massive revival of protest art, writing, and theater.

As right-wing vigilante terror increased against blacks and the Left, counter-groups of the "armed defense" type were organized. These groups, left and right, frequently clashed in bloody street battles. The police could no longer cope with the number of demonstrations and counter-demonstrations, so they relied more heavily on new technological innovations, like special gases. This resulted in escalation, as private and public armies began to experiment with counter-measures.

At the root of this chaotic picture was the simple fact that the B.L.F., various student "new left" groups, and even groups on the right had real problems which the government was not able to solve. The more militancy there was, the more real reforms were resisted by Congress; the more reforms were resisted, the more militant the protests became. Any semblance of "consensus" politics had disappeared by 1973. In the 1974 elections, no party would have a working majority in Congress.

Augmenting the "real" problems were those stemming from the protracted guerrilla warfare of the B.L.F. It became impossible to distinguish the causes of problems—the disruption of society by the B.L.F. and by the counter-militancy of the right, became indistinguishable from other causes, and from each other. There was an increasing clamor among middle-class Americans for a strong man to lead the country out of disaster. White radical groups vacillated between preparing for an underground existence, packing bags for Canada, engaging in electoral activity to counter the right, and trying to build broad "united fronts" to stop fascism.

On July 4, 1973, the Black Liberation Front held a "Congress of Black Americans for Home Rule" in Harlem. The Minutemen scheduled a march on Washington. The Huks took Manila. Black troopers of the 98th Airborne mutinied and destroyed two airbases. The Chief Justice of the Supreme Court and the Ambassador to the United Nations both resigned and flew to Switzerland. After turning the defense of the capital over to General Westmoreland, the President moved quickly to appoint a bi-partisan commission "to investigate and make recommendations . . . including the basic causes and factors . . ." [9]

*

The outcome is open; such a development has never occurred in Western, urban, industrialized society. The prognosis, perhaps fantastic, is not impossible given what we find in many strata of the population: a resistance to giving up anything in order to solve problems. Problem-solving *does* require some surrender of vested interests. Failing that, structural strain will increase, with collective behavior appropriate to historical circumstances. At this point, the logical and historical next step for the urban black, after proto-political activities such as rioting, would seem to be some kind of paramilitary action.

The options for the black urban guerrilla are these: (1) Insurrection now, with nearly certain repression and a catastrophic setback for any black protest movement. (2) A gradual build-up of subversion, with the possibility of total repression at virtually any point, resulting either in an insurrection of desperation or in an insurrection at what the rebels deem to be the culminating point of the subversion of the society. (3) The possible defeats of both of those insurrections —the first, because it is an insurrection of desperation and is not calculated to win, the second as the result of defeat in what is virtually a civil war. (4) Victory in the civil war, and the creation of (in all probability) some sort of interracial regime along authoritarian-leftist lines (authoritarian for reasons discussed in Chapter 3).

If the road to urban revolution is to be anything but an adventure, it will begin with terror and sabotage (assuming the exclusion of democratic processes as a feasible strategy). As soon as these methods become organized by secret societies, however, the terrorist groups are susceptible to infiltration and provocation—this is what can destroy the revolution at its inception, not search and seizure missions or concentration camps. But in a larger sense, guerrillas cannot be suppressed unless the problems that create them are dealt with effectively, for guerrillas will always be replaced by other guerrillas as long as the problems of oppression remain.

The ultimate answer to urban insurrection, or to the potential for it which lies in gradual subversion beginning with terror, is not the House Committee or the FBI or the "Civil Disobedience Squad." It is not Mace, foam, barbed wire, electronic eavesdropping, helicopters, or informers. It is solving problems.

CHAPTER SIX

THE NON-VIOLENT REVOLUTION

The revolutionist always suffers a tension between his revolutionary strategy and his day-to-day reform tactics. Revolutionists do advocate reforms—partly because so long as the system is capable of granting reforms, they are worth having, but more importantly: (1) to determine the limits of society's ability to reform itself, and (2) to enroll others in reform movements so that (a) they too can determine the limits of reform and the limits of society, and (b) they can be put in touch with revolutionary thought by working in the same milieu with revolutionists and thus become revolutionists themselves.

For this reason, classical revolutionists like Lenin worked in both the parliamentary and the underground arenas, often simultaneously. For Lenin the purpose of parliamentary work was not to pass legislation but to use parliamentary structures for subversive purposes, primarily to educate and organize for revolution. So Hitler wrote, "We know that no election can finally decide the fate of the nation . . . we know that in these elections democracy must be destroyed with the weapons of democracy." [1] And, at the other end of the revolutionary spectrum, Eldridge Cleaver, in a May 6, 1968, interview in *Peace and Freedom News,* stated that electoral politics "would be only an organizing tool . . . because this whole political system is so rigged . . . We only entered the political arena in order to destroy the status quo."

Classical reformers, on the other hand, attempt to persuade and move present rulers, and make real attempts at legislative reform because they believe that society as it is can be made to work better. Those who have a reform strategy (as distinct from the revolutionist's use of reform as a *tactic*) involve themselves in the politics of polite dialogue and gentlemanly pressure from within the government, and, in a society that is still functioning relatively well, electoral appeals based on moderation and consensus. In fact, it is not unusual for revolutionists, as they use the tactic of reform, to become more polite and de-emphasize their Marxian, conflict-oriented politics: the tactic gradually, almost imperceptibly, becomes the strategy, the means becomes the end. This has happened, for example, to the German Social Democratic party, and even to the French and Italian Communist parties. One of the main reasons for this gradual switch is that usually the society is still able to give reforms—the reform tactic pays off concretely, and the revolutionary strategy seems more and more chimerical.

The strategy of revolution is based on a long-range assumption that appeals and pressures will be useless, and that society will eventually falter, thereby creating a more fertile ground for guerrilla and insurgent activity. A revolutionary movement cannot, therefore, hold to this pessimistic assumption while living comfortably with the successful achievement of reforms. The movement must decide: shall it appeal to government or bring it down? Lacking such a decision, the movement creates contradictory signals both to the general population and to the government. The civil rights movement, which has within it both non-violent and guerrilla elements, is now in such a situation. In effect, the representatives of society do not know which wing to respond to, and so they respond first to one, then to the other, thereby adding to the confusion in the movement. Faced with this seesawing of policy from repression to minimal reforms, the movement deepens its own ambivalence about society, thus reinforcing the confusion of the government—and so on.

Once the road to insurrection has begun (by terrorism, for example), it is difficult to continue reform politics as a viable alternative. For one thing, the terrorists will begin to regard the reformers as renegades. On the other hand, the government can undermine the attraction of a violent solution to some degree by continuing to institute reforms—this is the argument for the "two-war" strategy, despite its other disadvantages. There is, for all revolutionists, a distinct "before" and "after" which are separated; tactically the revolutionist must decide at a particular point when to switch from reform appeals to insurrection. In the "before," the reform means, while oriented to the revolutionary ends, are not themselves consistent with the ends, that is, they are not revolutionary. Only in the "after," when tactics have changed to insurrection, are the means and the ends consistent.

A non-violent movement can, however, overcome that tension. It can *both* appeal to government *and* propose to overthrow it, simultaneously and openly. Its pressure to subvert takes the form of civil disobedience rather than terror, so that participants can both hope to better present society and change it fundamentally, at the same time. Unlike the violent strategist, the non-violent practitioner sees means and ends, the present and the future, as being dialectically interrelated. The means he uses are themselves revolutionary; thereby they create a qualitatively different end than that of the reformer who uses present-day, bourgeois (corrupt) means, or the violent revolutionist who at some point must cut himself off completely from legal means and work for a cataclysmic change in the future. Only in the non-violent revolutionary movement can a participant behave both "civilly" and subversively at the same time, hence the term "creative disorder" as opposed to the destructive disorder which is the prerequisite for a takeover by a violent revolutionary group. The key to the revolutionary content of non-violence (even though a particular tactic or campaign may not involve a conscious revolutionary intent) is in its method or style: its openness, trust, refusal to inflict physical or psychological injury on opponents, orientation to converting rather than beating opponents, and its internal decision-making by consensus, all symbolize a truly different (and revolutionary) departure from all other political methods and styles.

Insofar as government is concerned, the non-violent revolutionary movement presents a unified concept so that government cannot be confused by the contradiction that comes from parliamentarism plus terrorism. The state can, indeed, vacillate between repression and concession, but not because it is getting a confusing message—more likely it has not yet made up its mind, or is weakening; that is, it is a vacillation similar to the kind seen in governments confronted with a full-scale guerrilla war (not a situation in which reformers are still in action).

I raise this issue and emphasize the non-violent strategy because the viability of conventional reform politics is increasingly in question. But the alternatives, for many people, are equally untenable: become a guerrilla, or drop out. Unconventional non-violent revolutionism may be a way out.

RESISTANCE, RISING, REVOLUTION

Earlier in this book I distinguished among underground movements, risings (unplanned), and the protracted struggle of a revolutionary group, beginning with terrorism and sabotage and culminating in a planned insurrection when the regime has been so weakened by preceding tactics that a small push will suffice to overthrow it. The same schema can be applied to non-violence.

We begin with proto-political non-violence: passive resistance to oppression (non-cooperation, withdrawal from interaction) already takes place in a myriad of situations, in the form of such behavior as malingering or "goldbricking"; "pathological" behavior such as refusal to seek work, talking back to bosses and then quitting, reporting late for work, and absenteeism (deliberate, or resulting from real or imagined illness); and small-scale sabotage such as pilfering, overconformity to rules (resulting in work slowdowns), and so forth.

More political but not yet consciously revolutionary non-violence includes withdrawal tactics such as strikes, and intervention tactics such as sit-ins. These are not revolutionary in intent because they are oriented to specific reforms (for example, integration of a particular facility) without regard to long-range strategy. Nor is the strike (even the general strike) necessarily revolutionary, as we have seen, unless it is tied to a long-range political strategy. This is quite different from violent proto-political and proto-revolutionary behavior; by definition violence, because illegal and directed against the state (even in the form, say, of banditry), cannot directly help to create reforms. Those who use violence are by definition revolutionary, though they may not realize it. They have already made the break from society. Those who use non-violence are also revolutionary, *but not by definition of the state*—only by their method. They can continue to work in reform areas so long as this method is feasible.

Proto-revolutionary non-violence increasingly takes the form of a wide-ranging series of efforts by citizens to reassert decision-making power (especially over governmental bureaucracies) through the use of direct action. It is probably not necessary to go into great descriptive detail. On May 23, 1965, the *New York Times* summarized such developments in these words: "Civil rights, Vietnam and other major issues have led to a rising tide of demonstrations around the country. But another type of demonstration has also been on the increase. In community after community, local problems have been bringing into the streets ordinary citizens, often housewives, who normally don't 'take to the barricades.' . . ."

A brief survey of such direct-action situations would include protests against: traffic arrangements, the destruction of green belts, nature preserves, and historical landmarks by highway or urban renewal work, the employment of topless waitresses, low pay for doctors at public hospitals, high food prices, the eviction of staff and patients from a neighborhood hospital for non-payment of rent, and the refusal of hospitals to admit fathers to the delivery room. These are chiefly protests against lack of power, rather than efforts to "seize power" through the creation of dual or parallel institutions. Such protests, involving a wide variety of political points of view, seem destined to increase in number as information on "how to do it" spreads in middle-class reform circles.

But such activity, whether in the field of civil rights or peace, or in less directly political areas such as urban planning or saving trees, is not still consciously revolutionary. It is not directed at fundamental changes in the social order, and it is not oriented to a seizure of power and the establishment of a new government and society.

Roughly parallel to the idea of the short-term rising, appearing spontaneously and doomed to suppression by a powerful modern police apparatus, are non-violent or a-violent attempts to take power by means of strikes, seizures of buildings, marches, and demonstrations. Having inadequately subverted society beforehand, having failed to disarm the opposition (as well as failing to arm in whatever fashion the revolutionary forces themselves), such "confrontations" are doomed in the same way that violent urban insurrections are doomed. Often they are defensive, like the insurrections surveyed earlier, or are undertaken for symbolic purposes. Sometimes they are partially violent, or take place together with violent tactics (Czechoslovakia in August 1968 is an example). Sometimes they are parts of resistance movements rather than outright attempts to take power, such as the non-violent aspects of the Dutch, Danish, or Norwegian resistance movements during World War II. But a sudden attempt to take power non-violently is perhaps even more foredoomed than a sudden violent attempt, so long as the state is still viable.

The Pentagon demonstrations of October 21 and 22, 1967, serve as a good illustration of this kind of strategy. A great number of persons (estimated at somewhere between 100,000 and 200,000) marched to the Pentagon following a rally at the Lincoln Memorial Mall on Saturday afternoon, October 21. Perhaps most of these people crossed the fences set up to protect the Pentagon on that occasion, and surrounded the building with the idea of "confronting the warmakers." The Pentagon's immediate access ways were protected by some 2,500 federal marshals, District of Columbia police, and soldiers, with airborne units in reserve. Several thousand demonstrators managed to break through troop lines or scale the Pentagon front wall so as to get directly to the doors of the building. After several charges by troops, and massive arrests, the last two hundred demonstrators occupying "illegal" ground were arrested at midnight, October 22.

The tactics of the sponsors of the demonstration, once the crowd arrived at the Pentagon, were unclear; everyone was permitted to do pretty much what he wished. Some sat down to confront the troops guarding the building, others engaged in dialogue with them, still others yelled at them. Some charged the troop lines and broke through; others (Norman Mailer, for example) were arrested early while they were symbolically trespassing. Some demonstrators were non-violent, others a-violent, still others violent in response to the varying tactics of the marshals and soldiers. These included simple arrests, clubbings, the use of gas, and, on several occasions, a considerable degree of brutality.

The demonstrators considered the confrontation a victory—on what grounds it is not entirely clear. About seven hundred were arrested, but imprisonment did not seem to be an objective. Fraternization with the soldiers apparently resulted in some of them refusing to move against the crowd and even in some attempts to "go over" to the demonstrators, but these were extremely few. There were some lapses in military discipline, but in the main the soldiers behaved according to orders. The Pentagon was certainly not closed down, although its operations on October 21 were probably curtailed. The "war machine" was not disrupted. The impact of the demonstration on the general public (via the media) in terms of an image of the peace movement was generally negative, given the press's tendency to emphasize the violent and "hippy" aspects of the mixed tactics. Possibly the soldiers learned something about the peace movement—but different soldiers confronted different types of demonstrators, so they learned different things, not all of them positive. And possibly some demonstrators learned to know the reality of armed power by being victims of it.

Despite the obvious fact that an armed military organization, given discipline and orders, will use any violence on the part of demonstrators as an excuse for extreme retaliatory violence (so that even violent defensive responses by demonstrators are used as a provocation to destroy demonstrations), most American peace demonstrators did not learn from the Pentagon experience what the Czech population knew when the Russians invaded in August 1968. Instead, the same sponsors prepared still another a-violent, mixed-tactic confrontation with armed force for the Chicago Democratic Convention in that same month. Once again police and soldiers used the occasion as an excuse for massive arrests and brutality, although the news media this time placed the brunt of the blame on Chicago's brutally overreacting police force.

The inability of demonstrators to fraternize effectively when using a mixed bag of tactics, including cultural symbols guaranteed to provoke maximum hostility in frightened soldiers (and media audiences), such as Viet Cong flags; their inability to get the cooperation of functionally important groups such as trade unions (for example, in preventing troop movements against them); and their inability to sustain over time whatever disruption they have created, suggests that these attempts are useless from a revolutionist's point of view. They simply play into the hands of the Establishment. Far better to use smaller numbers of people, well-disciplined in a unified tactic, to create a series of disruptions in scattered places, in a "hit-and-run" guerrilla fashion, thus keeping the government in constant turmoil. The "educational effect" of watching police-state tactics on television seems to vary with the attitude the watcher brings with him; if he is already pro "law-and-order" or anti-demonstration, he will see only confirmation of his attitudes.

THE NON-VIOLENT GUERRILLA

This brings us to what might be called "protracted" non-violent conflict, roughly analogous to the long-range guerrilla war. As in guerrilla war, it seems to be true that ". . . revolutions are not, in fact, made by revolutionaries . . . The thing itself is caused by the persistent stupidities and brutalities of government . . . Even the Marxists have long since tacitly recognized this, and having wearied too long for the day when the inherent contradictions of their opponents' system would result in proletarian revolt, have come to place their undiminished faith in guerrilla or civil war . . ." [2] Assuming, then, that the society continues to be largely viable, and that for whatever reason the kind of protracted urban subversion suggested in the previous chapter is not desirable, how might a non-violent revolution be developed? Further, how might it be developed in such a way as to minimize the organization of counter-revolutionary forces which might defeat or repress it?

In guerrilla warfare the first stage includes the organization of terror-and-sabotage groups. At this stage, "revolutionary forces . . . are careful not to take any sort of military action that would give the forces of the established government reason for concerted counter-action." [3] Only later is there a major effort to organize armed bands. The non-violent revolution would have to unfold in a similar way. Small-scale "creative dislocations" and strikes by functionally important groups would have to be the initial steps. "Creative dislocations" might include slowdowns, blocking troop trains and induction stations, surrounding officials and preventing their mobility (to go home or to an office), picketing in the suburbs (à la Saul Alinsky), blocking armed forces and corporation recruiting on campuses, and the like. All of these things are being done now, but each has been invested with such great importance that when an event is suppressed, it is looked on as a defeat (or, sometimes, as a major victory). In a realistic non-violent conflict these disruptions would not be allowed to become major confrontations; they would be highly disciplined and completely non-violent in order to cast the enforcement agencies into disrepute. So long as demonstrators use violent tactics in any way, police can function; so long as confrontations are maximal, the military can function. This functioning can be undermined, though not eliminated, by the use of non-violence.

Whenever possible, small-scale disruption would be combined with strikes. It is difficult to believe that the Poor People's Campaign in Washington, in 1968, could have been so easily ended by riot police had black people working in government agencies called a strike. The unified demonstrations in Washington also were a tactical error. Small-scale non-violent harassment of individual congressmen would have been more effective (and harder for police to handle) than single large demonstrations. But this of course implies a well-disciplined non-violent army, one which under those circumstances would have been difficult or impossible to achieve.

Non-violent guerrillas would try to tie up some functioning part of society. After the murder of Martin Luther King, Jr., there was some talk of black workers striking, but this became pointless when everyone was given the following days off. Yet such groups as factory workers, welfare workers, and school-teachers, acting in concert and by surprise, can create chaos in an urban area, as we have seen after such relatively minor incidents as a power failure and a garbage collectors' strike. But such efforts would have to be short term and coordinated. Selective non-cooperation, disruption, and strikes would go on until the morale of the government was lowered and then, in theory, total non-cooperation (a general strike) could bring about total collapse.

These tactics have been developed in a general strategy known as "civilian defense," which is a non-violent way of dealing with an invading army. They have not specifically been applied to the strategy of revolution. In civilian defense, "The grand strategy of non-violent resistance . . . is based upon selective non-cooperation with the machinery and purposes of the invasion . . . today, there may be a strike at a

Gary steel mill, tomorrow a slowdown at a Camden shipyard, next week a crippling transportation halt in San Francisco . . . ," until the invading army's ability to deal with these situations is undermined. "The aim . . . is . . . to so affect the will of the invader's troops and agents that they become unreliable . . ." [4] The plan implies a unified population to start with, rather than a minority setting out to create a revolutionary situation. But there is no inherent reason why this could not be tried. As in the case of violent conflict, however, the non-violent revolution might not ever get to the "takeoff" point if the regime allows sufficient reforms to maintain a viable society.

THE NON-VIOLENT CENTER

With initial, small-scale acts of non-violent guerrilla conflict goes the equivalent of the guerrilla *foco,* the non-violent training center. Schools, exercises in non-violent action including role-playing, and other kinds of training programs would be essential. They would help to develop non-violence as *the* strategy and tactics of the movement—for, while a mixed violent-nonviolent strategy is possible, it creates a disunity which will enable the opposition to use one wing against another—as in fact is happening in civil rights today.

Besides special schools (on the model of the old Brookwood Labor School, the Highlander Folk School, or the Upland Institute, now called the Martin Luther King Jr. School for Social Change), small-scale cooperative communities run on non-violent principles (there is one in Voluntown, Connecticut), and institutes which carry out practice maneuvers (Grindstone Island, Canada), the non-violent guerrillas would have to set up para-"military" units. On an informal and uncoordinated basis, such units already exist. The Committee for Nonviolent Action, now merged with the War Resisters League, for years functioned as such a group, but solely on the issue of war. There have been others, notably the "Committee for Nonviolent Revolution" in the fifties and the "Peacemaker" group. But these have all maintained their separate identities and idiosyncracies. They have never formed the action arm of anything that can be called a movement.

The colleges and universities are among the more logical locales for the non-violent guerrilla foco, as Berkeley and Columbia have demonstrated. For non-violent guerrilla purposes, the university is ideal for creating cadres of dedicated people who will be able to move into strategic milieus after graduation. Such trained revolutionists can permeate American social institutions even though they may constitute only a small minority of college students—after all, 5 per cent of college students (the estimated normal percentage of real activists on campus) is 300,000 people! As the university trains people to man the status quo, key persons within university life (some professors, student organizations, key people in nearby communities) could train students to know how to act as non-violent guerrillas within the major institutions of society. Even on campus there are opportunities for such individuals to engage in limited actions, both for training purposes and in concert with off-campus resistance activities.

But could not such groups be infiltrated by spies and provocateurs in the same way as violent groups? And could they not be suppressed in a like manner? Furthermore, given the need for coordination and para-"military" organization, would such activity not suffer from the same tendency toward oligarchy seen in violent underground movements?

It is true that "civilian defense organization could also be secret and hierarchical. [But] how far non-violent defense would require regimentation would depend . . . on the kind of non-violent campaign planned . . ." [5] I do not think one must go to Jerome Frank's extreme and say that the military is "the only group with sufficient knowledge of organization and discipline to train and lead the civilian population in this type of combat." [6] A truly non-violent group, acting for the most part openly, and holding open discussion on most or all tactics, would not need to be spied upon, and discussion would tend to undermine provocateurs. So long as action is legal, or, if not legal, openly (civilly) disobedient, no secret command network would be required. The need to coordinate activity would necessarily lead to organization, hence to some oligarchy perhaps, but not nearly to the degree required by a truly clandestine group.

The complications arise when non-violent guerrilla activity is combined with violent activity. "So long as those willing to resist . . . have only a choice between violent action and the *idea* of non-violent resistance, they have in reality no choice at all." [7] Violent activity therefore tends to appear first, and once it appears it is hard to "transarm" to non-violence. As one military man has observed, "If you have the circumstances in which . . . a successful guerrilla war can take place, you already have in the country a large number of people who want it to happen." [8] This is one of the biggest problems for non-violent practitioners.

NON-VIOLENT RESISTANCE

Apart from civilian defense against an alien invader, and non-violent non-cooperation and obstruction as part of a wider underground movement against an occupation army, little has been written about the movement which might follow the small-scale beginnings of non-violent revolution outlined above. One might suppose that as more people came into the movement, activity would intensify; the least committed would be involved in non-cooperation tactics (strikes, stay-at-homes or "Hartals," boycotts or partial boycotts, tax refusal, malingering, absenteeism, slowdowns, refusal of honors and positions, including boycotts of committees, and so on). On a somewhat more committed level would be tactics of protest including marches, picketing, vigils, fraternization, and street-corner meetings. The least likely to be legal, hence the most dangerous activity, requiring the most committed and experienced people, would be the tactics of intervention: sit-ins, reverse strikes (in which people carry out tasks which they are not supposed to do, even illegal ones), and obstruction of various kinds. One expert, Gene Sharp, lists seventy-two forms of non-cooperation, thirty-six kinds of protest, and sixteen ways of intervening.[9]

While long-term resistance, as in conventional guerrilla warfare, makes more sense than a premature attempt to take over a government, this does not mean it is without danger. "Civilian defense . . . would result in widespread death and injury to the resisters . . . though certainly far less than in the event of a thermonuclear war," is the overall judgment of a Quaker study group.[10] The same judgment applies to the non-violent revolution. During World War II the Germans were not familiar with passive resistance (when it occurred); but today's armed forces are far better prepared to cope with non-violence, both technically and psychologically. Advocates of non-violence, one British military specialist reminds us, "are inclined to overlook the fact that its main successes have been obtained against opponents whose code of morality was fundamentally similar, and whose ruthlessness was thereby restrained . . . The only impression it seems to have made on Hitler was to excite his impulse to trample on what, to his mind, was contemptible weakness . . ." [11] If we accept the premise of the black revolutionists in this country, namely, that we live in a racist society, less ruthlessness can hardly be expected.

As non-violent resistance to a system expands, small-scale passive resistance combines with larger demonstrations, and non-violent guerrilla intervention increases so as to disrupt social institutions. Through fraternization, opponents are in theory disarmed, neutralized, or even converted. "Strategies and methods which cause maximum strain and therefore over-stretch" the opponent's resources are adopted.[12] Increasingly, strikes are redirected from reform demands to more funda-mental demands for participation in decision-making and changes in organizational structure and control. Workers' councils might be set up as para-organizations in plants, agencies, communities, and universities. Ordinary police duties might be taken over by citizens' groups (as in France during the strikes in the spring of 1968) as police become occupied with demonstrations.

A SCENARIO

It might be interesting to try to depict the course of a non-violent insurrection, along the lines of the two scenarios in the previous chapter. Actually, "role-playing" experiments in "civilian defense" have already taken place. In a thirty-one-hour experiment on Grindstone Island in Ontario Province, Canada, in August 1965, thirty-one non-violent "defenders" had to deal with six "armed" men representing a United States–supported "right-wing Canadian government [which had] occupied major portions of the Canadian heartland . . ." At the end of the experiment, thirteen of the defenders were "dead"; the participants "concluded that the experiment had been a defeat for nonviolence." [13] A working party of the American Friends Service Committee, on the other hand, de-veloped a scenario (not an experiment) in which the United States successfully "transarmed" to non-violent national defense in the face of a thermonuclear threat.[14]

*

In 1969, after the inauguration of the new President, several pacifist groups coalesced to form the "League for Nonviolent Revolution." The League issued a manifesto stating that democracy was effectively at an end in the United States, and that conventional channels for reform and change were no longer practicable. The League called for open, non-violent resistance to the new administration "and its collaborators throughout all social institutions," until such a time as "America's imperialism abroad and colonialism at home" was ended and a non-violent, communitarian society was created. "The day of petition is over; the day of intervention is here," the manifesto declared.

Initially the League took no overt, illegal actions. Passive resistance and training were the chief tactics during the first year of the new movement. Training centers, both college-based (especially in the Quaker colleges) and independent, were organized. Tax refusal finally became a significant movement when the Southern Christian Leadership Conference backed it. This resulted in the imprisonment of Reverend Ralph Abernathy. Draft refusal became so widespread that Congress was forced to let the Selective Service law lapse, and the country then moved toward an entirely volunteer army.

The summer of 1970 was "Resistance Summer." Nearly a half-million college students were involved in community and peace organizing; most of them adopted a "digger"-style economy (living in cooperative communities from what they could get free) for the summer. Resister-diggers held at least a dozen massive marches in rural areas to "capture" crops destined to be destroyed by farmers due to the bumper harvests. The commodities were carried and trucked into ghetto areas and distributed free. That fall, the returning students literally took over dozens of colleges and, together with sympathetic faculty, ran them "free university" style. All became training centers for further non-violent resistance and revolution.

By this time several hundred thousand alumni of the Students for a Democratic Society were working in Establishment institutions. Their "Movement for a Democratic Society" gradually began to influence professional organizations and white-collar unions, especially those of teachers, social workers, government employees, and college professors. A one-day general strike to support Christmas amnesties for conscientious objectors and other movement prisoners was so effective that all major cities in the East came to a standstill. A five-day strike, supported in many cases by black industrial workers, succeeded in obtaining a presidential order withdrawing the last American troops from Southeast Asia, except for those attached to United Nations peacekeeping forces. Another five-day stoppage early in 1971 got the "freedom budget" passed. Intermittent strikes and slowdowns achieved the revamping of several city educational and welfare systems.

All of these events were seen as extremely threatening, despite their non-violent aspects, by the nation's political and military leaders and by some segments of the business world, which began to notice increasing demands for "participation" in decisions affecting both white- and blue-collar workplaces. The Republican party demanded "law and order," and strikes and other demonstrations began to face increasing police harassment and vigilante persecution. Legal restrictions prevented the M.D.S. from running candidates for public office. More and more laws were passed forbidding various student and worker-power activities. There was a massive crackdown on hippies and "love-ins," and most "digger" activity was made illegal. "Jail-ins," not popular since the early 1960's, once again became part of movement strategy.

By the spring of 1971, strike after strike tied up most governmental agencies. The President could find no one from outside the Establishment to attend his annual White House Conference (all participants were over fifty). Massive resignations occurred in both governmental and corporate organizations still involved in defense production, and the League for Nonviolent Revolution had to set up a placement service for these people. Literally thousands of non-violent actions, ranging from "guerrilla theater" interruptions of commercial films, plays, and lectures, to large-scale consumer boycotts and massed street sit-ins to prevent the movement of troops against strikers, took place. There was considerable fraternization between non-violent revolutionists and police and soldiers. Increasingly, soldiers and police refused to fire, or even use gas, on demonstrators, all of whom were trained to show good humor and friendliness at all times.

The League, the M.D.S., and various black organizations met on July 4, 1971, to set up a "Congress of Free Americans." This Congress proceeded to elect a "government" and pass "legislation." It declared the regular government "illegal." The City of New York, which six months earlier had disarmed its police and "transarmed" to non-violent methods, declared its allegiance to the Free Congress. Its entire delegation to the United States Congress resigned and took places in the Free Congress. Wall Street was at a standstill—leading businessmen did not know whether to laugh or panic. The country faced a non-violent insurrection and was seemingly unable to come to a consensus on how to deal with it; only the ultra-right continued to attack, militarily, the actions of the League and the M.D.S. But on every side they were confronted by committees—factory committees, student committees, neighborhood committees, non-violent action committees. In effect, the structure of society now revolved around functioning committees rather than bureaucracies or government. The committees *were* the government, and they answered only to the Free Congress. Washington's problem was not that it confronted an insurrection as much as that it was *irrelevant* to an insurrection. For the first time in decades, Washington, D.C., was losing population.

The development of the non-violent revolution to this point had not been easy, nor was revolution assured even in late 1971. First, black organizations had not yet accepted non-violence as a strategy; joint actions repeatedly involved some violence, and in some cases had to be canceled. There were also violent-prone elements (especially from the "old left," plus some "Che" and "Mao" adherents) in the M.D.S. Each time violent repression by police or armed forces was responded to violently, there was a setback, and the psychological "warfare" of non-violence vis-à-vis various opponents was undermined. Each time "trust" had to be rebuilt so that fraternization could once again proceed.

Many Americans saw the non-violent movement as in some sense immoral, threatening, or violent (some of the news media helped along this view) and turned to an ultra-right movement which, many observers believed, would resist with violence any attempt to bring about fundamental changes in the country. It was an open question whether the revolution would be able to maintain its non-violent strategy under such extreme conditions.

*

This scenario is far more outlandish than those of the preceding chapter, admittedly. Still, if society fails to function, revolutionary movements do arise. The fact that so far in history most of them have been violent, or have in the course of events become violent, does not mean that such a development is inevitable.

FROM RESISTANCE TO REVOLUTION

Non-violence is more difficult to use in a positive revolution than in defensive resistance. Ultimately, revolution must force a government out of power and replace it. The long-range perspective of non-violent revolution, just as in the case of the violent protracted guerrilla war, is that while the revolution begins with a minority, it must end with the conversion or neutralization of a majority. This means, assuming that Black Liberation continues as a leading feature of the American revolutionary perspective, that an interracial movement with interracial demands must ultimately be created. Recent developments in Black Power circles indicate that this is already being planned. In a recent interview, Eldridge Cleaver, for example, says:

> . . . the rhetoric of the black power movement was developed as a tool for waging this purge of white control of black organizations. So we feel that this has virtually been achieved . . . we see no reason for continuing this stance of isolation one from the other . . . let's get together and move in a common fashion against a common enemy . . . As long as we remain isolated we must remember that we subject ourselves to a very vicious power structure that takes advantage of all division . . .[15]

But against whom is this revolution to be directed, and what social group is to take power in society? This is the critical issue which American revolutionists have yet to confront. For it is now obvious that the majority of the working class and virtually the entire middle class are either satisfied or fear the changes proposed by the left—the structural strain which is the necessary prerequisite to revolution is missing for most people. This, of course, is the reason for guerrilla activity, whether violent or non-violent. It is to create the strain, in a sense, artificially. But there are no guarantees as to the political direction a movement created in response to strain may take. Those affected by the strain initiated by the guerrillas are just as likely (perhaps more likely) to go in a counter-revolutionary or fascist direction as they are to join the revolution.

The rationale suggested by proponents of Chicago-style confrontations is that no other tactic has worked, that the system is no longer able to effect reforms proposed by conventional means. In fact, it seems to me that proposed reforms have been ignored because they are not considered desirable or necessary by vast numbers of people. That is, the system functions *so well* that change is now unable to attract significant support. Confrontation politics, whether violent or non-violent, seems more a sign of desperation resulting from failure to convince the people of a need, not a symptom of the system's imminent collapse.

The forces of revolution in the United States, therefore, are likely to be limited for some time to come to a portion of the black population (that portion which, by the way, is least likely to choose a non-violent solution), the most alienated students, some of the disaffected in white-collar life, and, perhaps, a limited sector of the industrial working class, especially that portion involved in democratic opposition groups within some of the more oligarchic trade unions. Revolutionary ideology will have to spread from these groups to those whose lives are basically satisfying. This is not a promising perspective so long as the government is able to keep society running on a more or less even keel. And if it is not, the demands of the ultra-right that "law and order" be "enforced" may impose such repression on the advocates of change (non-violent though they may be) that the resistance movement may be crushed.

Furthermore, the techniques of non-violence are not limited to good people. "Passive resistance," as Thomas Schelling points out, "has been notoriously the technique by which non-integrating Southern states have frustrated the federal government . . .," [16] and there is no reason to suppose that such tactics cannot be used by rightists. Reverend James Lawson, addressing the 1961 annual meeting of the Southern Christian Leadership Conference, proposed training a non-violent army of two thousand to eight thousand volunteers which could accomplish "the complete wresting of political power from the hands of white supremacists in the states of the Deep

South and its transfer . . . to governments representing the whole population." [17] But counter-measures along the same lines can be taken, for example in the form of refusing bank credit or jobs to known leftists, and establishing blacklists. And such "passive resistance" could become more demonstrative. One can envision, for example, a non-violent training center surrounded by rightist demonstrators to prevent entry or exit; leaders of the non-violent movement constantly harassed by telephone calls and haunted by rightist demonstrators; rightists taking over the more repressive functions of police busy with anti-demonstration tasks (vigilante anti-crime units, and so forth); rightists tying up a university and provoking police intervention. It is easier, of course, to think of ways of tying up government than of defending government against such groups. Yet one can even envision a situation in which anti-government and pro-government groups confront each other relatively non-violently. For example, how would non-violent guerrillas be able to seize a government building or a university building (in order to disrupt the functioning of the institution) if that building is being protected by a mass of non-violent defenders?

This leads to another consideration: that of the mixed violent-nonviolent strategy. Civilian defense against an outside invader is not necessarily congruent with complete nonviolence. Non-violent resistance (or rather, a-violent resistance) to a foreign invader has almost always been closely linked to violent resistance, including terrorism and sabotage. Non-cooperation has often been used with military methods against an occupying army. An example was the guerrilla war against the British in Cyprus.[18] One can make a good argument, in fact, that in any attempt to subvert society, the best mix is one of selective terror and large-scale non-violent action. This of course presents other problems such as those associated with all violent clandestine organizations. And there is little doubt that a mix is to the advantage of a violent defending force. In an unequal struggle where revolutionists are faced by superior force, only an iron non-violent discipline has even a chance of disarming the opponent, neutralizing him so he will not fire, and so on. To mix in violent responses is not only futile but suicidal, for it will only confirm the attitude of the violent defender that his enemies must be responded to violently. Rioting and looting also confirm these attitudes, for they often force the government to move in troops and react violently to the violent situation, when otherwise it would have been more difficult (though perhaps not impossible) for a repressive strategy to be carried out.

A non-violent movement, if it is to remain so, requires a larger number of participants to give its members some sense of safety, than does a violent movement. That is, if participants are required to defend themselves non-violently against the repressive measures of government or the coercive measures of vigilante "ultra" groups, there must be extensive protective and supportive measures available, including such tactics as non-violent intervention between a mob and an intended victim, a strike to prevent transportation of army units to suppress a demonstration, and other logistical measures like feeding and housing people fired from jobs. This is because non-violence is open, so that active participants are immediately marked and become targets. The participant in a clandestine violent movement need fear only being caught in the act, which is far less likely than in a non-violent episode, or being turned in by informers.

If such larger-scale protective measures are not available, the non-violent cadre will find itself easily slipping into a strategy mix, as did the civil rights workers of the South who, lacking non-violent protection against rightist terrorists, began armed defense, which became the prelude to much current talk of urban guerrilla warfare. Failing a massive campaign to organize non-violent protective measures, the use of armed defense to support non-violent resistance in its earlier stages can be expected.

The prognosis for a non-violent revolution is scarcely more promising than that for a violent outbreak. It is true that either violent or non-violent revolutionary activity, or some mix of them, could undermine our social institutions enough to subvert them and create a "civil war" or revolutionary climate. But such developments all presuppose an increasing inability of society to meet the needs of functionally important segments of its population. It is doubtful whether, even with the added input of violent or non-violent dislocation, sufficient structural strains can develop to neutralize or disaffect enough of the population so as to prevent society from functioning. Even if such a condition could be achieved by such partially external (hence artificial) means, the development of a counter-revolutionary, rightist movement is just as, or even more, likely than a leftist, radical-type movement. And rightist movements have no hesitation, historically, in mixing violent and a-violent tactics. The most likely development, I believe, in reaction to attempts by the left to disrupt and subvert society, will be a large-scale fascist movement, the forerunners of which are already apparent on the political scene.

This does not mean that the radical left is responsible for the growth of the right, or that the left ought therefore to disappear quietly on the assumption that the right will then also do so. Rather, both left and right, to the extent both flourish, do so in response to similar social strains, varying their response according to social class and historical circumstance. But then, once each appears, both ends of the political spectrum by their appearance alter the social environment, increasing its strains and reacting one to the other in an inseparable fashion.

Little revolutionary theory today is based on the premises of a majoritarian revolution in response to strain, plus relevant ideology. Rather it is based on the assumption that a minority may have to carry the revolution through, as in a rural guerrilla epoch. But even if this were to happen, on whose behalf would the urban insurrectionist rule? The rural guerrilla takes power, as I have suggested, with the backing of the peasantry, but on behalf of a new class of bureaucrats. The urban guerrilla, assuming that he is able to neutralize the bulk of the population, takes over with the backing, presumably, of the most alienated sectors of society, the urban equivalent of the peasantry once it becomes revolutionary: the lumpenproletariat (including the unemployed and underemployed black population), alienated intellectuals, some industrial workers, and some white-collar employees. These are, together, *more* able to rule in their own name than are peasants, but they have differing interests and as a group are not a functional class. That is, they do not, by virtue of their work, control anything. Upper management does; so does the industrial working class as a whole, and even the white-collar class as a whole; but these do not back the revolution as a whole— on the contrary, most do not participate in it and in fact probably oppose it. The revolution rules in their name, but they do not rule. In their absence from effective participation in the revolution, the same thing happens that happens in a peasant-based revolution: gradually the leaders of a minority-led revolution become a new bureaucracy, a new class of rulers. A violent minority revolution would hasten the process, but a non-violent one would not necessarily preclude it.

Revolutionists should be reminded of the words of Engels, written in 1850:

> The worst thing that can befall a leader of an extreme party is to be compelled to take over a government in an epoch when the movement is not yet ripe for the domination of the class which he represents . . . he is [thus] compelled to represent not his party or his class,

but the class for whose domination the movement is then ripe. In the interests of the movement he is compelled to advance the interests of an alien class, and to feed his own class with phrases and promises . . . Whoever is put into this awkward position is irrevocably lost.[19]

Modern society is ripe for the domination of bureaucracy, in the absence of a revolutionary working class. Perhaps the leader of a minority revolution is not himself irrevocably lost, but his revolution is.

CHAPTER SEVEN

REACTIONS, BLACK AND WHITE

Today's city is the most vulnerable social structure ever conceived by man. At one time designed to serve an agrarian society as a center for its products and as a focal point for commerce, it is now declining in importance to the nation's commerce and industry; at the same time it becomes more and more dependent for its survival on resources beyond its effective control. In the United States, moreover, this decline in importance to the society as a whole is coupled with population trends that make the city increasingly the home of the black and the poor. Thus, while the city is vulnerable to dislocations caused by insurgency warfare, hence jeopardizing such societal decision-making centers as may remain in it (for example Wall Street), at the same time anyone dislocating it also jeopardizes the very population which he is trying to help by revolutionary methods. Put plainly, the urban guerrilla cannot disrupt society by disrupting the city, unless he also inflicts heavy suffering on his own people. And if he seizes the city, he seizes that which is at present most expendable, most bankrupt, most backward (economically and governmentally speaking) in our society, with the possible exception of Appalachia.

The vulnerability of the ghetto population is becoming evident to militant black leaders.[1] But the city's vulnerability to paramilitary attack is also obvious. In Chicago, on the South Side, "every fourth street is commercial; arsonists could set off fires in the principal white-owned businesses of each street, thereby occupying the fire and police departments while saboteurs spread out over the city to derail trains (most of which run through the ghettos), blow up power plants, and despoil water systems." [2] In Detroit, the East Side has several "vital" installations, including electricity, water, Chrysler, and Parke Davis pharmaceutical plants. In Philadelphia, ghetto areas command the communication route from Washington to New York (except by air), border the industrial northeast and southwest of the city, and virtually surround the University of Pennsylvania–Drexel Tech complex (including a major railway and post office center).

THE ARMS RACE

Increasingly, police are equipping themselves to handle urban disturbances.[3] Elaborate contingency plans, including computerized data-control systems, carefully trained tactical units from federal down to local police levels, and the latest in counter-insurgency weaponry (helicopters, gases, Stoner assault rifle systems, counter-sniper teams, armored vehicles, electronic snooper devices), are now a normal part of a city's budget. The tactical "improvements" developed in the last several years make earlier army and police manuals on riot and mob control look as relevant as Orville Wright's first airplane. And the sheer economic weight of such repressive measures to urban governments and to society more generally is fantastic and clearly out of proportion to its alleged benefits.

Even by adding up what is known about individual communities, it is difficult to get an accurate figure as to the cost of this repression to society, considering only preparations, not actual enforcement in a real situation. But the remarkable rise in the prices of "security industry" stocks may be one index. One expert has estimated the size of the "law enforcement market" at about $2.5 billion per year, which, almost needless to say, is more than the 1968 federal budgetary appropriation to the Office of Economic Opportunity. (This does include about $1.2 billion for "protective service companies" such as Pinkerton's, which are only partially devoted to anti-riot or related activities.) [4]

Blacks are arming, the police are arming, and the ultra-right is arming. "All over the U.S.A. the John Birchers, the Minutemen, the States Righters, the Nazis and Ku Klux Klanners are arming and training for total warfare against our people. . . . The Afroamerican hasn't got a chance in the U.S.A. unless he organizes to defend himself," says Robert F. Williams.[5] "We have taken off the kid gloves with these elements who cause riots," says the police chief of Tampa, Florida. "Are you ready now to prepare yourself for the next one? Or will you be forced to stand helplessly by because you were unprepared to defend your home or neighborhood against bands of armed terrorists who will murder the men and rape the women?" asks a Detroit white group.[6] "——— knows the answer is law and order, not weak-kneed sociology. ——— doesn't bail them out, he puts them in. He doesn't apologize for them—he fights violence and puts a stop to it," reads a full-page political advertisement for an assistant district attorney seeking a Republican nomination for Congress in June 1968.

"Preparations" are accompanied by dire prophecies about a second civil war, decades of urban turmoil, and a hopeless division of the races for generations to come. At the same time, government and business agencies alike continue to explore and expand the field of "human relations." There are endless meetings, conferences, and training exercises in "defusing" the urban problem. While actual legislation to deal with problems amounts to little, there is no dearth of good will, and brotherhood messages continue to pour fourth across Kiwanis tables, and down from pulpits.

ESTABLISHMENT STRATEGIES

Police repression tactics can be viewed as part of a "two-war" strategy being waged by urban establishments and by the national political and social power structure to "save the cities." The other side of that war is the so-called "war on poverty." In the same way that a two-war strategy is fundamentally unworkable in an underdeveloped colonial setting, so is it unworkable in the colonial setting of the American ghetto, for the military side of the strategy undermines the social side, even assuming that the social side is sound—which it is not. The war on poverty, with all its auxiliaries, functions basically to maintain the ghetto in its colonial position vis-à-vis the American power structure. It co-opts ghetto leaders and amalgamates them into the lower echelons of the Establishment. The exploited condition of the mass of ghetto dwellers remains little changed so far.

If the costs of riot control are added to other measures needed to keep the American city afloat (welfare, renewal, highways, and so on), it should be clear that cities are expensive to the power structure. A clever establishment might well choose to flee the cities as do businesses and many middle-class individuals. The Stock Exchange has even spoken of moving from Wall Street. The movement of our nation "toward two societies, one black, one white—separate and unequal" mentioned by the President's Commission on Civil Disorders,[7] would thus be accelerated, and a kind of "black power" would be created.

It is clear that the Establishment is divided on this strategy. Business elements who talk of building up black businesses in the ghetto seem more and more to be opting for an abandonment of the city by business in the direct sense, preferring to exert indirect control through investment in the "internal colony." Sometimes this can even be done with anti-poverty funding assistance, and in the guise of militant black power. In Philadelphia, Reverend Leon Sullivan's Opportunities Industrialization Center, a job-training facility supported partially by parishioners and partially by the federal government, expanded in early 1968 to found a plant, Progress Aerospace Enterprises, Inc., which is "all-black-initiated, owned, and administered." It is a subcontractor of General Electric for $2.6 million, and of the Department of Labor (for job training) for another $522,000. Banking support was provided by Philadelphia's First Pennsylvania Company.[8] In this way, some capital generated by the community and some invested indirectly from the outside by private and government sources combine to increase the pool of "native" entrepreneurs and at the same time create a stable auxiliary to white business in the black ghetto, free from the threat of black riot.[9]

This strategy is welcomed by some black power advocates and explains their flirtations with political figures who seem to be recommending a "neo-colonialist" strategy. Interestingly enough, an identical conflict seems to be underway in terms of our international policy. The British and French long ago learned that the "two-war" strategy is far less effective in maintaining economic hegemony over a colony than the strategy of neo-colonialism, which involves giving political independence. Political leaders advocating a Vietnam "reappraisal" seem to be moving in a similar direction—and it is suggestive that some of these same leaders lean toward strengthening some aspects of black power.

On the other hand, particularly in the political establishment, the more conventional "two-war" strategy continues to receive support, and a battle continues to rage between those who prefer repression and those who emphasize the "other war"; this conflict also replicates some Establishment views concerning Vietnam. Both domestically and internationally then, we have "hard-liners," "soft-liners," and "reappraisers," that is, colonialists, liberals, and neo-colonialists. But this conflict within the establishment is not always obvious. It is more latent than manifest, and on the surface it will often appear in the guise of confusion and "mixed strategies." For one thing, reforms of the "other war" kind often overlap with reforms of the neo-colonialist kind; Progress Aerospace Enterprises is that kind of mixture, as are many ghetto endeavors in which "self-help" and "maximum feasible participation" by the community are combined with attempts to seek equal job opportunities within white-run institutions.

A micro-model of this problem can be seen in the Negro college. Here Afro-American culture, history, languages, and the like are taught in a context which also prepares black students to take their places in white graduate schools, businesses, and welfare institutions. In miniature, this context mirrors the identity crisis of the American black and reflects the strategy-crisis of the American white establishment in dealing with the black ghetto.

Relatively moderate black power demands can therefore be

absorbed without basically changing the ghetto. It may be possible for the system to amalgamate even more radical "cooperative self-help" schemes, for, as Harold Cruse suggests, "American capitalism's dynamic . . . can take every one of what [Robert F. Williams] calls the essential demands of 'our people' and use them to buy off and absorb every militant wave of the entire Negro movement, as fast as they emerge." [10]

The function of neo-colonialism as an Establishment strategy is obvious: it is cheaper and makes for more stability. What, then, is the function of repression?

Since repression makes little economic sense, there must be other reasons for it. Partly, repression is related to the antiquated nature of urban government, to which the neo-colonialist strategy is another reaction. That is, because the police department exists, it is required to maintain order even if that maintenance is economically unsound. A white police department which acts as an occupying force in the ghetto makes little rational sense. Black communities can police themselves and in fact govern themselves efficiently. But this latter view does not prevail in Establishment thinking; the culture-lag conditions that prevail in urban government still dictate a "two-war" strategy which, by definition, involves police repression as one of its components. The police, like welfare institutions, see black power (even under neo-colonial auspices) as a real threat to their own power, and jobs. Repression therefore functions to preserve jobs and power.

A second function of repression is psychological: urban police act on behalf of many in society who are racist and fear blacks. A violent movement, or one which for any reason can be perceived as violent (even though falsely), permits society to rationalize the evasion of ghetto problems. A non-violent movement, on the other hand, at one time blocked off this kind of response by refusing to let society off the hook of responsibilty. "The non-violent movement force[d] right-minded people to confront the real issues of social justice. Were the movement violent, many people would evade the real issue of justice by getting 'hung up' on the violent *means*. Riots give people an excuse they've been looking for." [11]

More concretely, violence is directly functional to certain police forces that seek to destroy black militance altogether (which is why, in recent months, black militants have sought to evade direct confrontations in which they would lose, a lesson learned at great expense by every guerrilla movement in the world). But the image of violence must be preserved in order to rationalize these tactics. The best way to assure that is to act as if the present movement were violent, react to it violently, and thereby create a self-fulfilling prophecy as the movement tries to defend itself. The fear of blacks causes arming, by both police and private citizens; arming causes blacks to arm; this creates more fear, and so on—an arms race, in short.

THE ULTRAS

In general, police represent the "military wing" of a "two-war" strategy. In many localities and at the national level, Establishment thinking continues to prefer "law and order" under its own auspices, rather than the erratic social controls imposed by ultra-rightist groups. Symptomatic of this preference was the police defense of a pacifist camp in Connecticut against an armed Minuteman attack in August 1968; similar police actions against plans of Minutemen and, in the South, the Klan had taken place before. Establishment political figures today continue largely to espouse a viewpoint opposed to extra-legal methods because such methods undermine the stability of the system.

The police wing of the establishment itself does not always share this perspective, however. More and more, it would seem, police see the moderate wing of the establishment as being partly, or largely, responsible for the instability of the system by refusing to let the police "do their job," that is, apply police powers rigorously to minority ethnic and leftist political groups. Attacks on the Supreme Court are part of this approach. Hence, rather than representing one wing of a "reform" strategy, police sometimes become a part of an outright ultra-rightist repression strategy. The repression of the California Black Panthers suggests such a variation, although this normally takes the form of citizen vigilante action. It is not difficult to see how this can lead to a perception of the police as an occupying force. "If white America is the mother country and black America is the colony, then the white police of Oakland are not police at all, but occupation troops . . . then the question of [Huey] Newton's [Panther minister of defense, convicted of manslaughter] guilt or innocence according to white law is really irrelevant: he is a political prisoner charged with defending the integrity of his people . . ." [12]

There is a time when law enforcement agencies no longer enforce the law against the ultra-right, or against proto-counter-revolutionaries. In many communities that time is fast approaching. The facts are evident on every hand: "Parallel to the rise of the new Radical Right since 1960 . . . there has been a sharp increase in the interest shown in weaponry, military tactics, 'self-defense,' . . . stimulated . . . by the rise of 'guerrilla' bands such as the Minutemen . . ." [13] Domestic arms production for private use is now about two million rifles and shotguns per year, and almost 600,000 handguns, and imports add another 1.2 million units.[14] Private white groups, arising partly in response to the threats they perceive from black insurgency, as well as from the failure of the police to "enforce" the laws (as these groups see it), are growing in number. In Detroit, for example, six organizations issued a joint call urging citizens to defend their homes against "armed terrorists"; the head of one of them has also helped break up civil rights demonstrations and disrupt interfaith church services. Reverend Albert Cleage, a leading Detroit Black Nationalist, responded to such activities this way: "The ranges of the shooting clubs are packed; the city is way behind in processing gun registrations. So, naturally, any black man who can get hold of a gun is getting hold of it." [15]

Many law enforcement agencies are infiltrated by the right and work hand-in-glove with it, by no means exclusively in the South, as the Panther case suggests. Law agencies throughout the country, up to the federal level, have been harassing not only militant black groups but more conventional direct-action civil rights groups, as well as left-wing groups, for years. In such an atmosphere rightist terror groups become bolder and begin to operate more freely to subvert the rights of others. Germany in the 1920's offers a classic case of such subversion; observers have pointed to a disquieting parallel in this country, in this era of political assassinations. (To speak of locally controlled gun legislation under such circumstances is to disarm the left and the black militants, preventing them from using armed defense as a deterrent to rightist terrorism—and leaves the ultra-right untouched.)

Hate activity has always been in long supply on the American political scene. Anonymous telephone calls, poison-pen letters, disruption of meetings, attempts at character assassination, blacklists, and the like are not new. But while it is not easy to make comparisons, rightist activity probably has not been so widespread since the uncertain times of the 1930's as it is today. A recent letter published in a respectable newspaper is an indication of the depth of this attitude:

> Like millions of others, stunned, shocked, and appalled by the recent tragedy, one wonders "who is next," and too, when will the obvious (if drastic) steps be taken to deport all deportable Communists and to put Red fellow

travelers and their like in concentration camps or under strict surveillance?

Not even the most naive or knavish can now deny that both the late President Kennedy and his brother Robert were murdered by Red rats. If the lawfully constituted authorities lack the courage and common sense to act (and but fast) an alarmed, outraged and long suffering populace might. Let's stand up and be counted, and "if that be treason, make the most of it." [16]

Small wonder that Rap Brown has reportedly called for white leftists to bring him guns, and if they couldn't do that, give money to somebody who *can* buy a gun.

THE FUNCTIONS OF REFORM

Reform includes both the "other side" of the "two-war" strategy, and the neo-colonialist strategy, for both intend to make concessions in order to preserve the essence of the system. The "other war" is oriented to the creation of a black elite which will take its place in the lower echelons of the white power structure; neo-colonialism aims at creating black enclaves which will be politically and economically stable subsegments of the dominant white system. The ability of the system, so far, to adapt to various pressures from the black community has led Harold Cruse to the verdict that ". . . the American social dynamic has the built-in persuasion to bend all so-called revolutionary inclinations into the reformist groove . . . [and] . . . buy off all the ghetto rebels with consummate ease." [17]

A social system has what might be called a reform potential, which is an index of its viability. Reforms are, in other words, a constant test of a system's parameters. Its ability to produce a particular reform in the face of pressure creates for it an outpost, as it were, against revolution. If there are no out-posts, it is either because the system has not yet been tested or because they have fallen, in which case the fortress is open to attack and the system is ripe for revolution.

As long as a reform is demanded and the system *can* give it, it will be given, provided enough pressure is applied. But if the system *cannot* give a particular reform (because it strikes too closely at some *fundamental* aspect of the system, as its leadership sees it at the time), then we know its point of weakness. The revolutionist looks for those limits of a system to press an attack. To paraphrase Guevara, so long as government can maintain the appearance of viability (through establishing boundary points by specific reforms), revolutionary struggle cannot be successfully promoted, "since the possibilities of peaceful [conventional] struggle have not yet been exhausted."

Furthermore, despite strong arguments that paramilitary and non-violent struggle can undermine a system and create a revolutionary climate (that is, so that the outposts of re-form fall), this has really never happened. Nowhere has sig-nificant revolutionary warfare begun except where the regime had already refused (hence, for whatever reason, was unable) to make reforms. Every guerrilla outbreak has begun only after some colossal break in the system—for example, refusal to hold elections, large-scale purges, arrests and shootings, the alienation of some significant group by refusing to permit it any access to some (even limited) power, massive repression of some potentially revolutionary minority group, and so forth.

This is why repression helps a revolution. It forces people to the conclusion that reforms are no longer obtainable, hence to a break with the system. Any establishment worthy of the name will try to avoid such a situation at any cost short of surrender. Any revolutionist worthy of the name will constantly test a system to force it to give every reform it can, and then, when it cannot or will not give any more, to the surrender point—"up against the wall."

Once revolutionary warfare has broken out, attempts to reverse the trend (for example, through the "two-war" strategy) are very difficult if not impossible. In exceptional cases, usually involving an insurrection prematurely manufactured by adventurers, or even outsiders, the establishment can still hope to deal with the situation by setting up outposts of reform so as to promote a perception by citizens that the system is indeed viable.

In the contemporary American situation, many see the system as ripe for revolution because one set of outposts has been seemingly overrun. It would appear that at the local level, at the state level, and even to some degree at the national (at least congressional) level, the limits of reform in the political arena have been reached at least for the next few years. These reforms have proven inadequate when they have not actually worsened the situation (through false assumptions and promises, bad planning, or corruption). Adequate reforms are blocked by a nationwide political system which increasingly proves unresponsive to society's problems.

Moreover, the political system appears less and less suited to be a lever for change. At the state and local levels, certainly, political parties seem to be the property of those in power and their cronies; they are organized to exclude participation by concerned citizens seeking reform. Patronage continues to be the primary function of politics and patronage in turn functions to sabotage those reforms that are instituted. As a result, reform elements in society (from business to the poor) seek ways to bypass or sidestep the political system. Neo-colonialism is an establishment response designed to create reforms when they cannot be pushed through "normal" political channels.

CO-OPTATION

Co-optation is perhaps one of the most important ways any system copes with strain. By co-optation I mean "the process of absorbing new elements into the leadership or policy-determining structure of an organization as a means of averting threats to its stability or existence." [18] In concrete terms, establishment organizations attempt to bring leaders of dissident or opposing power groups into a relationship with the establishment so that the dissidents are forced to accept some responsibility for establishment decisions. In this way, radicals are forced to become more "responsible" and their opposition is "de-fused." This is done by giving dissident groups a minor voice in decisions of secondary importance. An older-fashioned method, still sometimes effective, is to add dissident names to letterheads or to large boards or committees—usually so large they are ineffective decision-making bodies to begin with. The concept of "maximum feasible participation" of the poor on local anti-poverty boards is a form of co-optation; the poor rarely constitute more than one-third of such boards and in any case are divided among themselves and organizationally inexperienced. But the tactic fosters an illusion of participation and undermines protests that local boards are unrepresentative.

So far, enlightened establishment leaders have been remarkably successful in the co-optative strategy chiefly through the war on poverty. The slowdown of this war in the face of repressionist tactics, and the culture lag in political institutions, has promoted establishment support of limited black power as an alternative form of co-optation.

The relatively new phenomenon of "responsible militancy" is a part of neo-colonialist tactics. Whether this takes the form of using militant blacks as deputy sheriffs, as in Chicago, or of black-power-oriented rock-singer James Brown cooling off a Boston riot after the King assassination (leading, significantly, to a White House invitation for him), or of "responsible" Tim Still or "supermilitant" LeRoi Jones using Chamber of Commerce money to form "trouble squads" to keep Newark from exploding, is irrelevant. Only the Black Panthers have at this point not been made, in some way, an adjunct of the system. This is probably because of the incredible stupidity of the repression-oriented power structure in Oakland. On the surface, many of the Panther demands are no more revolutionary than those of other militant groups which have by now become partners of more enlightened local white establishments.

CHAPTER EIGHT

WHAT STRATEGY FOR REVOLUTION?

In the course of this brief study of insurrection and revolution, I have tried to establish several broad points:

(1) Peasant-based revolutions seem historically to end in the dictatorship of the "new class."

(2) Unaided urban insurrections, given modern technologies of counter-insurgency warfare, are doomed.

(3) A protracted war, whether rural- or urban-based, cannot by itself disable society enough to create a revolutionary situation; rather, the society must suffer from sufficient strains so as to allow revolutionary activity to "make sense." The protracted war can add to that strain, but it cannot create sufficient strain by itself.

(4) In a modern, industrialized, metropolitan setting, the

subversion of society by strain, aided by violent or non-violent guerrillas, is very likely to end in a right-wing, counter-revolutionary dictatorship.

(5) Even if successful, and even if non-violent, such a revolution, representing an active minority only, runs a strong risk of ending in a dictatorship of "the new class," although this risk is hardly a sufficient reason for a revolutionist not to try anyway.

(6) So far, the establishment in the United States, working both through traditional integrationist and neo-colonialist black power reform strategies, has been able to co-opt black protest and avoid serious revolutionary threats to itself.

Yet there is little question that large segments of our society (even though a minority) are in serious trouble and do not share in that society. Moreover, there is little doubt that traditional reform measures (including the "war on poverty," which has already become traditional), will be inadequate for solving the problems of that minority (which includes the black population, increasing numbers of underemployed and unemployed working-class whites, marginal farmers, and alienated students). This is particularly true given the vested interests of local political establishments, plus at least some powerful economic interests, in blocking such reforms and repressing their advocates.

Furthermore, even the neo-colonialist strategy of permitting limited or perhaps even fairly extensive black political autonomy over the ghetto, augmented by black economic power of a private or cooperative nature, and black cultural institutions, in the long run will not meet the needs of the black population. For no matter how autonomous the black ghetto, it will continue to exist as a dependent sub-system of the dominant white American political and economic system. Even the extreme of nationhood for all Afro-Americans would permit independence only as part of an American bloc and would therefore keep the black population in a semi-colonial status—though perhaps not as colonized as at present.

It is conceivable that our society will be able to muddle through, or zigzag in and out of a semi-permanent crisis for many years without either solving its basic problems or confronting a revolution, because of its ability to maintain outposts of reform. How many years depends on such relatively unknowable factors as the ability of the American economy to cope with international trade and monetary problems, the rate at which automation and cybernation increase the number of alienated, the shrewdness of revolutionary movements in posing successful challenges to the system, and the ability of the establishment to cope with such challenges.

This suggests that there will continue to be some kind of a pre-revolutionary movement in America. It is difficult to be precise about what form such a movement will take—by implication I have predicted that its most likely form will involve violence. For some time to come it will be a dual movement, with white radicals in one separate wing and black militants in another, with occasional cooperation on specific issues and with sporadic conflict over tactics and strategy.

But it is time now to suggest not only what *may* be but also what *ought* to be. In the main, this book has not been involved in advocacy, although an author's viewpoint always creeps in, most particularly when he attempts to deny it. In terms of a personal statement, then, what shape should the movement take? In general I agree with Christopher Lasch [1] that the political left must create a party of its own, not primarily for electoral activity as such, nor even to register protest votes or try to act as a lever on the other parties. Rather, such a party must try to "introduce socialist perspectives into political debate, to create a broad consciousness of alternatives not embraced by the present system, to show both by teaching and by its own example that life under socialism would be preferable . . ."

What Lasch is getting at is not politics for the sake of getting elected to office, but a creation of the revolution by means of "institutions that would parallel existing structures of government" so that people can find ways to function that are fulfilling and non-alienating. In a way he is saying what the advocates of non-violence say when they argue that the movement, because it is non-violent, begins to create a revolutionary spirit even under an oppressive system.

Such a party or movement (the beginnings of which are all around us, in such forms as Students for a Democratic Society, the Free University movement, Advocacy Planning, and the many ideas associated with the concept of "participatory democracy") has a large potential constituency even now, though it does not constitute a majority. It includes, as Lasch points out, people located in "the professions . . . suburbia, in the ghetto, and above all in the university, which more than any other institution has become a center of radicalism." (Which is why the university is the logical foco for the non-violent guerrilla if society should come to that point.)

But how will such a movement be able to translate the hostility of the majority into neutrality at worst, alliance at best? If revolution comes from strain, the strain created by automation and cybernation may create populations susceptible to revolutionary demands. Both the white-collar class (gradually to be dislocated or unemployed, or at best facing drastic changes in the nature of work) and the blue-collar class are vulnerable; the ghetto is already alienated; and the university, suffering the strain of being asked to serve man and bureaucracy at the same time, will become more vulnerable as an institution, and its members more alienated.

The new party must be oriented to both community-level issues and wider national and international issues, attempting to link all of these to the wider perspective of revolutionary change in the world and the need for qualitive change in individual lives. It must be a party inside of which an individual can change his own life while testing the system's outposts of reform.

This means that such a party must reflect a genuine movement, from the bottom up. It cannot be slapped together by an *ad hoc* group at the top. It must represent, in a genuine way, local, neighborhood, campus, and work-place groups which are already functioning along anti-establishment lines. Furthermore, it must seriously orient itself to the problems of white- and blue-collar workers, for these are the only classes which, due to their relationship to the functioning of modern society, have both the potential for making a revolution and the capability of carrying it through on a democratic basis.

If the system proves resilient enough, such a political movement can force qualitative changes upon it. I doubt that this will be the case. Given the pressures of a revolutionary age, reform will probably prove inadequate, and crises will beset the system in a far more serious way than at present. Then, in the classical way of all rotting social structures, its people will have to choose: revolution or counter-revolution, democracy or totalitarianism? At that moment, the revolutionary movement must be sufficiently developed and intelligent enough to provide a viable revolutionary and democratic alternative.

A revolution cannot be artificially induced. A new society cannot be born before its time. To attempt to induce it prematurely, before the old order has sufficiently prepared the way, is adventurism, and is almost inevitably bound to result either in a counter-revolutionary fascist society or in a revolutionary dictatorship which destroys the goals for which the revolution was undertaken. The liberation of mankind, as the Marxian saying has it, must be the work of mankind itself, must be majoritarian and democratic. No elite, whether violent or non-violent, can substitute.

NOTES

INTRODUCTION

1. Crane Brinton, *The Anatomy of Revolution*, New York, Prentice-Hall, 1938; Hadley Cantril, *The Psychology of Social Movements*, New York, Wiley, 1941; Rudolf Heberle, *Social Movements*, New York, Appleton-Century-Crofts, 1951.
2. Georges Lefebvre, *La Revolution Francaise*, Paris, Peuples et Civilisations, 1951; C. L. R. James, *The Black Jacobins*, New York, Vintage, 1963.
3. Gustave LeBon, *The Crowd*, New York, Viking Press, 1960; first published in 1895.
4. Raymond Aron, *The Century of Total War*, Boston, Beacon Press, 1955; Hannah Arendt, *The Origins of Totalitarianism*, Cleveland, World, 1958; Lewis Coser, *The Functions of Social Conflict*, Glencoe, Ill., Free Press, 1956.
5. Che Guevara, *Guerrilla Warfare*, New York, Monthly Review Press, 1961; Regis Debray, *Revolution in the Revolution?*, New York, Grove Press, 1967.
6. T. N. Greene, ed., *The Guerrilla—and How to Fight Him*, New York, Praeger, 1962.

7. Feliks Gross, *The Seizure of Political Power*, New York, Philosophical Library, 1958.
8. Rex Applegate, *Crowd and Riot Control*, Harrisburg, Pa., Stackpole, 1964.
9. Martin Oppenheimer and George Lakey, *A Manual for Direct Action*, Chicago, Quadrangle Books, 1965.
10. *Ramparts,* March 1968; Gary Wills, *The Second Civil War*, New York, New American Library, 1968 (parts published in *Esquire,* March 1968). See also Mike Klare, "Urban Counterinsurgency: An Introduction," *Viet-Report,* Summer 1968, "A Special Report on Urban America in Revolt."
11. Chalmers Johnson, *Revolutionary Change*, Boston, Little, Brown, 1966.
12. Ralph Linton, "Nativistic Movements," *American Anthropologist,* vol. 45 (1943), 232.
13. Anthony Wallace, "Revitalization Movements," *American Anthropologist,* vol. 58 (1956), 265.
14. Chalmers Johnson, *Revolution and the Social System*, Stanford University, Hoover Institution, 1964.
15. Mikhail Zetlin, *The Decembrists*, New York, International Universities Press, 1958.
16. Theodore Abel, *Why Hitler Came into Power*, New York, Prentice-Hall, 1938, p. 348.
17. Harry Eckstein, ed., *Internal War*, New York, Free Press, 1964, p. 6.

ONE: COLLECTIVE BEHAVIOR

1. Ralph H. Turner and Lewis M. Killian, eds., *Collective Behavior,* Englewood Cliffs, N.J., Prentice-Hall, 1957, pp. 3–11.
2. Johnson, *Revolution and the Social System,* p. 23.
3. Anthony Wallace, *Culture and Personality*, New York, Random House, 1964, p. 144.
4. C. Wendell King, *Social Movements in the United States*, New York, Random House, 1956, pp. 13, 15.
5. Allan Silver, "The Demand for Order in Civil Society: A Review of Some Themes in the History of Urban Crime, Police, and Riot," in David J. Bordua, ed., *The Police*, New York, Wiley, 1967, pp. 23–24.
6. Wilhelm Reich, *The Mass Psychology of Fascism*, New York, Orgone Institute Press, 1946, pp. 26–27.
7. More detailed discussion of social movement theory can be found in, among others, Turner and Killian, *Collective Behavior;* Neil J. Smelser, *Theory of Collective Behavior*, New York, Free Press, 1963; and Hans Toch, *The Social Psychology of Social Movements*, Indianapolis, Bobbs-Merrill, 1965.
8. E. J. Hobsbawm, *Primitive Rebels*, New York, Norton, 1965, p. 15.
9. Robert T. Anderson, "From Mafia to Cosa Nostra," *American Journal of Sociology,* vol. 71 (November 1965), 302–310.
10. For example, Peter Worsley, *The Trumpet Shall Sound*, London, MacGibbon and Kee, 1957; Vittorio Lanternari, *The Religions of the Oppressed*, New York, Knopf, 1963; Frederick Engels, *The Peasant*

War in Germany, Moscow, Foreign Languages Publishing House, 1956, first published in 1850; and James, *The Black Jacobins.*

11. U.S. Department of Labor, *Labor Unionism in American Agriculture,* Bulletin #836, Washington, U.S. Government Printing Office, 1945.
12. Silver, in Bordua, *The Police,* pp. 23–24.
13. Tom Hayden, *Rebellion in Newark,* New York, Random House, 1967, p. 69.
14. Hayden, *Rebellion in Newark;* Robert Conot, *Rivers of Blood, Years of Darkness,* New York, Bantam Books, 1967; Russell Dynes and E. L. Quarantelli, "What Looting in Civil Disturbances Really Means," *Trans-action,* vol. 5 (May 1968), 9–14; National Advisory Commission on Civil Disorders, *Report,* New York, Bantam Books, 1968; *American Behavioral Scientist,* vol. 11 (March–April 1968), Special Issue on Urban Violence and Disorder; Irving L. Horowitz and Martin Liebowitz, "Social Deviance and Marginality," *Social Problems,* vol. 15 (Winter 1968), 280–296; Anthony Oberschall, "The Los Angeles Riot," *Social Problems,* vol. 15 (Winter 1968), 322–341; Stanley Lieberson and Arnold R. Silverman, "Precipitants and Conditions of Race Riots," *American Sociological Review,* vol. 30 (December 1965), 887–898.
15. Hayden, *Rebellion in Newark,* p. 70.
16. Harold Black and Marvin J. Labes, "Guerrilla Warfare: An Analogy to Police-Criminal Interaction," *American Journal of Orthopsychiatry,* vol. 37 (July 1967), 666–670.

TWO: THE COUNTRYSIDE VERSUS THE CITY

1. Leon Trotsky, *Permanent Revolution* and *Results and Prospects,* New York, Pioneer Publishers, 1965, first published 1905 and 1906.
2. Don Bacheller, "Guerrillaism, the Peasantry, and the N.L.F.," *Independent Socialist,* April 1968, pp. 19–20.
3. S. M. Lipset, "Democracy and the Social System," in Eckstein, *Internal War,* p. 269.
4. Mehmet Beqiraj, *Peasantry in Revolution,* Ithaca, N.Y., Cornell Research Papers in International Studies (V), 1966, 92.
5. Frantz Fanon, *The Wretched of the Earth,* New York, Grove Press, 1966.
6. Barrington Moore, Jr., *The Social Origins of Dictatorship and Democracy,* Boston, Beacon Press, 1967, p. 453.
7. Fanon, *The Wretched of the Earth,* pp. 145–152.
8. Guevara, *Guerrilla Warfare,* pp. 16, 17.
9. Greene, *The Guerrilla—and How to Fight Him,* p. 5.
10. *Ibid.,* p. 147.
11. Debray, *Revolution in the Revolution?*
12. James Petras, "Guerrilla Movements in Latin America—II," *New Politics,* vol. 6 (Spring 1967), 65.
13. See her *The Russian Revolution,* Ann Arbor, University of Michigan Press, 1961 (with *Leninism or Marxism?*), pp. 69–71.

THREE: THE LIMITS OF REVOLUTION

1. Moore, *Social Origins of Dictatorship and Democracy*, p. 492.
2. Norman Mailer, "The Steps of the Pentagon," *Harper's*, March 1968.
3. Moore, *Social Origins of Dictatorship and Democracy*, Epilogue.
4. Herbert Marcuse, *One-Dimensional Man*, Boston, Beacon Press, 1964, p. 256.
5. Alfredo Rocco, *The Political Doctrine of Fascism*, New York, Carnegie Endowment for International Peace, 1926, p. 10.
6. Hermann Rauschning, *The Revolution of Nihilism*, New York, Alliance Book Corp., 1939, p. 92.
7. Rocco, *Political Doctrine of Fascism*, p. 25.
8. Irving L. Horowitz, "Cuban Communism," *Trans-action*, vol. 4 (October 1967), 9.
9. Ted Gurr, "Urban Disorder: Perspectives from the Comparative Study of Civil Strife," *American Behavioral Scientist*, vol. 77 (March–April 1968), 50.
10. Fanon, *The Wretched of the Earth*, p. 73.
11. Abel, *Why Hitler Came into Power*, pp. 176, 179, 180.
12. Eldridge Cleaver, "A Letter from Jail," *Ramparts*, June 1968, p. 19.
13. Jawaharlal Nehru, *Toward Freedom*, Boston, Beacon Press, 1958, p. 69.
14. B. H. Liddell Hart, "Lessons from Resistance Movements—Guerrilla and Non-violent," in Adam Roberts, ed., *Civilian Resistance as a National Defense*, Harrisburg, Pa., Stackpole, 1968, p. 204.
15. Nechayev, quoted in Gross, *Seizure of Political Power*, p. 342.
16. Conor Cruse O'Brien, "Confessions of the Last American" (a review of Norman Mailer's *The Armies of the Night*), *New York Review of Books*, June 20, 1968.
17. Hart, in Roberts, *Civilian Resistance*, p. 203.
18. J. K. Zawodny, "Guerrilla and Sabotage: Organization, Operations, Motivations, Escalation," in *Annals of the American Academy of Political and Social Science*, vol. 341 (May 1962), special issue on "Unconventional Warfare," ed. by J. K. Zawodny, 15.
19. Gross, *Seizure of Political Power*, p. 343.
20. Andrew R. Molnar, William A. Lybrand, Lorna Hahn, James L. Kirkman, and Peter B. Riddleberger, *Undergrounds in Insurgent, Revolutionary, and Resistance Warfare*, Washington, American University, Special Operations Research Office, 1963, p. 184.
21. Oppenheimer and Lakey, *Manual for Direct Action*, p. viii.
22. Philip Selznick, *The Organizational Weapon*, New York, McGraw-Hill, 1952.
23. Brinton, *Anatomy of Revolution*, chap. 8.

FOUR: PARAMILITARY ACTIVITIES IN URBAN AREAS

1. An earlier version of a part of this chapter, with some ideas from Chapter 1, appears in Louis H. Masotti and Don R. Bowen, eds., *Riots and Rebellion: Civil Violence in the Urban Community*, Beverly Hills, Calif., Sage Publications, 1968.
2. Russell Rhyne, "Patterns of Subversion by Violence," *Annals*, vol. 341 (May 1962), 65–73. See also William S. Allen, *The Nazi Seizure of Power*, Chicago, Quadrangle Books, 1965.
3. William Worthy, "Anti-War Sabotage," reprinted from the *Boston Globe*, July 28, 1968, in Resist Newsletter #15, August 27, 1968.
4. Lucian W. Pye, "The Roots of Insurgency and the Commencement of Rebellions," in Eckstein, *Internal War*, pp. 157–179.
5. Gross, *Seizure of Political Power*.
6. Molnar, *Undergrounds*, p. 3.
7. *Ibid.*, p. 4, 7, 13.
8. Gross, *Seizure of Political Power*, p. 355.
9. *Ibid.*
10. Molnar, *Undergrounds*, p. 344.
11. *Proceedings of the Second International Conference on the History of the Resistance Movements*, Milan, Italy, March 26–29, 1961, New York, Macmillan, 1964, p. xxxiii.
12. *Proceedings*, p. 109.
13. Otto Heilbrunn, *Partisan Warfare*, London, Allen & Unwin, 1962, p. 180.
14. *Proceedings*, pp. 522–571.
15. *Ibid.*, p. 347.
16. *Ibid.*, p. 356.
17. *Ibid.*, pp. 361–362.
18. Gross, *Seizure of Political Power*, p. 357.
19. Robert F. Williams, *Negroes with Guns*, New York, Marzani & Munsell, 1962; Truman Nelson, *The Right of Revolution*, Boston, Beacon Press, 1968, pp. 86–87.
20. Harold A. Nelson, "The Defenders," *Social Problems*, vol. 15 (Fall 1967), 144–145.
21. Horowitz and Liebowitz, "Social Deviance and Marginality," p. 290; William W. Turner, "The Minutemen," *Ramparts*, January 1967, pp. 69–76.
22. Raymond Postgate, *How to Make a Revolution*, London, Hogarth Press, 1934, p. 142.
23. *Ibid.*
24. *Ibid.*, p. 138.
25. *Ibid.*, p. 145.
26. Peter Paret and John W. Shy, *Guerrillas in the 1960's*, New York, Praeger, 1962, pp. 57, 75.
27. Gross, *Seizure of Political Power*, pp. 356, 358.
28. Debray, *Revolution in the Revolution?*, p. 35.
29. Paret and Shy, *Guerrillas in the 1960's*, p. 76.

30. April 1968.
31. John C. Leggett, Richard Apostle, Al Baronas, and David Driscoll, "Total Cultural Revolution, Class-Racial Consciousness, and Current U.S. Insurrections," paper presented at the meetings of the American Sociological Association, San Francisco, August 1967, pp. 11–12.
32. *New York Times,* June 9, 1968.
33. Jerry Bornstein, "Question in Quebec: Who Will Take Power?," *Guardian,* September 21, 1968.

FIVE: THE BLACK GUERRILLA

1. *I. F. Stone's Weekly,* August 19, 1968.
2. Frank Jellinek, *The Paris Commune of 1871,* London, Gollancz, 1937.
3. O. Edmund Clubb, *Twentieth-Century China,* New York, Columbia University Press, 1964.
4. Gerd Korman, "The Setting," *New University Thought,* vol. 6 (March–April 1968), Special Commemoration Issue for the 25th Anniversary of the Warsaw Ghetto Uprising, 7.
5. Raul Hilberg, *The Destruction of the European Jews,* Chicago, Quadrangle Books, 1961, pp. 168–174.
6. Lewis M. Killian, *The Impossible Revolution: Black Power and the American Dream,* New York, Random House, 1968.
7. Robert F. Williams, quoted in Committee on Un-American Activities, U.S. House of Representatives, *Guerrilla Warfare Advocates in the U.S.,* Washington, U.S. Government Printing Office, 1968, p. 19.
8. Committee on Un-American Activities, pp. 57–58.
9. National Advisory Commission, *Report,* p. 534.

SIX: THE NON-VIOLENT REVOLUTION

1. Konrad Heiden, *Der Fuehrer,* Boston, Houghton Mifflin, 1944, p. 348.
2. D. J. Goodspeed, "The Coup d'État," in Roberts, *Civilian Resistance,* p. 36.
3. Alun Gwynne Jones, "Forms of Military Attack," in Roberts, *Civilian Resistance,* pp. 19–20.
4. American Friends Service Committee, *In Place of War: An Inquiry into Nonviolent National Defense,* New York, Grossman, 1967, pp. 49, 52.
5. Theodor Ebert, "Organization in Civilian Defense," in Roberts, *Civilian Resistance,* p. 289.
6. Quoted in William Robert Miller, *Nonviolence: A Christian Interpretation,* New York, Association Press, 1964, p. 109.
7. Ebert, "Organization in Civilian Defense," p. 257.
8. Jones, "Forms of Military Attack," p. 18.
9. A.F.S.C., *In Place of War,* p. 61.
10. *Ibid.,* p. 49.
11. Hart, "Lessons from Resistance Movements," in Roberts, *Civilian Resistance,* p. 206.
12. *Ibid.,* p. 209.
13. Theodore Olson and Gordon Christiansen, *Thirty-One Hours,* New London, Conn., Grindstone Press, 1966, pp. 1–2.

181 Notes

14. A.F.S.C., *In Place of War.*
15. *New America,* June 15, 1968.
16. Thomas C. Schelling, "Some Questions on Civilian Defense," in Roberts, *Civilian Resistance,* p. 307.
17. Miller, *Nonviolence: A Christian Interpretation,* p. 83.
18. Jones, "Forms of Military Attack."
19. Engels, *Peasant War in Germany,* pp. 138–139.

SEVEN: REACTIONS, BLACK AND WHITE

1. Fred J. Cook, "It's Our City, Don't Destroy It," *New York Times Magazine,* June 30, 1968.
2. William Barrow, "Chicago Regrets," *New Republic,* April 20, 1968.
3. Wills, *Second Civil War;* John Duffett, "Defending the State," *Guardian,* May 4, 11, 18, 1968; *Viet-Report,* Summer, 1968.
4. According to Leonard Sloane, *New York Times* financial writer, *New York Times,* April 15, 1968.
5. Harold Cruse, *The Crisis of the Negro Intellectual,* New York, Morrow, 1967, pp. 385–386.
6. Wills, *Second Civil War.*
7. National Advisory Commission, *Report,* p. 1.
8. *New York Times,* June 30, 1968.
9. Tom Hayden, in *Viet-Report,* Summer 1968, predicts that "white society will continue to encourage the growth of the classic 'comprador bourgeoisie' of blacks to administer the colony for the mothercountry." An interesting parallel in Quebec is that of the Mouvement Sovereignté Association which, according to Jerry Bornstein (*Guardian,* September 21, 1968), "proposes a form of neocolonialism for Quebec. The plan is to recognize and accept U.S. domination of the economy, and, shying away from nationalization, to develop small-scale industries run by the indigenous bourgeoisie to supply large U.S. companies."
10. Cruse, *Crisis of the Negro Intellectual,* p. 389.
11. Oppenheimer and Lakey, *Manual for Direct Action,* p. 120.
12. Gene Marine, "The Persecution and Assassination of the Black Panthers," *Ramparts,* June 29, 1968, pp. 37–46.
13. Arnold Forster, "Violence on the Fanatical Left and Right," *Annals,* vol. 364, (March 1966), special issue on "Patterns of Violence," 145.
14. *New York Times,* June 23, 1968.
15. Wills, *Second Civil War.*
16. *Poughkeepsie Journal,* June 18, 1968.
17. Cruse, *Crisis of the Negro Intellectual,* p. 549.
18. Philip Selznick, *TVA and the Grass Roots,* Berkeley, University of California Press, 1949, p. 259.

EIGHT: WHAT STRATEGY FOR REVOLUTION?

1. Christopher Lasch, "The New Politics: 1968 and After," *New York Review of Books,* July 11, 1968.

INDEX

A NOTE ON THE AUTHOR

Martin Oppenheimer grew up in New York and New Jersey and studied at Temple, Columbia, and the University of Pennsylvania. Formerly an assistant director of the studies program for the American Friends Service Committee, he has taught sociology at Bryn Mawr, Haverford, and Vassar colleges, and is now chairman of the Department of Sociology and Anthropology at Lincoln University in Pennsylvania. Mr. Oppenheimer's first book, *A Manual for Direct Action* (written with George Lakey), came to be highly valued by those engaged in non-violent protest in the late sixties, influencing students as far away as Berlin. He lives in Oxford, Pennsylvania, with his wife, Sally, and a daughter.

QUADRANGLE PAPERBACKS

American History

Frederick Lewis Allen. *The Lords of Creation.* (QP35)
Lewis Atherton. *Main Street on the Middle Border.* (QP36)
Thomas A. Bailey. *Woodrow Wilson and the Lost Peace.* (QP1)
Thomas A. Bailey. *Woodrow Wilson and the Great Betrayal.* (QP2)
Charles A. Beard. *The Idea of National Interest.* (QP27)
Carl L. Becker. *Everyman His Own Historian.* (QP33)
Barton J. Bernstein. *Politics and Policies of the Truman Administration.* (QP72)
Ray A. Billington. *The Protestant Crusade.* (QP12)
Allan G. Bogue. *From Prairie to Corn Belt.* (QP50)
Kenneth E. Boulding. *The Organizational Revolution.* (QP43)
Robert V. Bruce. *1877: Year of Violence.* (QP73)
Gerald M. Capers. *John C. Calhoun, Opportunist.* (QP70)
David M. Chalmers. *Hooded Americanism.* (QP51)
John Chamberlain. *Farewell to Reform.* (QP19)
Alice Hamilton Cromie. *A Tour Guide to the Civil War.*
Robert D. Cross. *The Emergence of Liberal Catholicism in America.* (QP44)
Richard M. Dalfiume. *American Politics Since 1945.* (NYTimes Book, QP57)
Carl N. Degler. *The New Deal.* (NYTimes Book, QP74)
Chester McArthur Destler. *American Radicalism, 1865-1901.* (QP30)
Robert A. Divine. *American Foreign Policy Since 1945.* (NYTimes Book, QP58)
Robert A. Divine. *Causes and Consequences of World War II.* (QP63)
Robert A. Divine. *The Illusion of Neutrality.* (QP45)
Elisha P. Douglass. *Rebels and Democrats.* (QP26)
Felix Frankfurter. *The Commerce Clause.* (QP16)
Lloyd C. Gardner. *A Different Frontier.* (QP32)
Edwin Scott Gaustad. *The Great Awakening in New England.* (QP46)
Ray Ginger. *Altgeld's America.* (QP21)
Ray Ginger. *Modern American Cities.* (NYTimes Book, QP67)
Ray Ginger. *Six Days or Forever?* (QP68)
Gerald N. Grob. *Workers and Utopia.* (QP61)
Louis Hartz. *Economic Policy and Democratic Thought.* (QP52)
William B. Hesseltine. *Lincoln's Plan of Reconstruction.* (QP41)
Granville Hicks. *The Great Tradition.* (QP62)
Dwight W. Hoover. *Understanding Negro History.* (QP49)
Stanley P. Hirshson. *Farewell to the Bloody Shirt.* (QP53)
Frederic C. Howe. *The Confessions of a Reformer.* (QP39)
Harold L. Ickes. *The Autobiography of a Curmudgeon.* (QP69)
Louis Joughin and Edmund M. Morgan. *The Legacy of Sacco and Vanzetti.* (QP7)
William Loren Katz. *Teachers' Guide to American Negro History.* (QP210)
Burton Ira Kaufman. *Washington's Farewell Address.* (QP64)
Edward Chase Kirkland. *Dream and Thought in the Business Community, 1860-1900.* (QP11)
Edward Chase Kirkland. *Industry Comes of Age.* (QP42)
Adrienne Koch. *The Philosophy of Thomas Jefferson.* (QP17)
Gabriel Kolko. *The Triumph of Conservatism.* (QP40)
Walter LaFeber. *John Quincy Adams and American Continental Empire.* (QP23)
Lawrence H. Leder. *The Meaning of the American Revolution.* (NYTimes Book, QP66)
David E. Lilienthal. *TVA: Democracy on the March.* (QP28)
Arthur S. Link. *Wilson the Diplomatist.* (QP18)
Huey P. Long. *Every Man a King.* (QP8)
Gene M. Lyons. *America: Purpose and Power.* (QP24)
Jackson Turner Main. *The Antifederalists.* (QP14)
Ernest R. May. *The World War and American Isolation, 1914-1917.* (QP29)
Henry F. May. *The End of American Innocence.* (QP9)
Thomas J. McCormick. *China Market.* (QP75)
George E. Mowry. *The California Progressives.* (QP6)
William L. O'Neill. *American Society Since 1945.* (NYTimes Book, QP59)
Frank L. Owsley. *Plain Folk of the Old South.* (QP22)
David Graham Phillips. *The Treason of the Senate.* (QP20)
Julius W. Pratt. *Expansionists of 1898.* (QP15)
C. Herman Pritchett. *The Roosevelt Court.* (QP71)
Moses Rischin. *The American Gospel of Success.* (QP54)
John P. Roche. *The Quest for the Dream.* (QP47)
David A. Shannon. *The Socialist Party of America.* (QP38)
Andrew Sinclair. *The Available Man.* (QP60)

American History (continued)

John Spargo. *The Bitter Cry of the Children.* (QP55)
Bernard Sternsher. *The Negro in Depression and War.* (QP65)
Richard W. Van Alstyne. *The Rising American Empire.* (QP25)
Willard M. Wallace. *Appeal to Arms.* (QP10)
Norman Ware. *The Industrial Worker, 1840-1860.* (QP13)
Albert K. Weinberg. *Manifest Destiny.* (QP3)
Bernard A. Weisberger. *They Gathered at the River.* (QP37)
Robert H. Wiebe. *Businessmen and Reform.* (QP56)
William Appleman Williams. *The Contours of American History.* (QP34)
William Appleman Williams. *The Great Evasion.* (QP48)
Esmond Wright. *Causes and Consequences of the American Revolution.* (QP31)

European History

William Sheridan Allen. *The Nazi Seizure of Power.* (QP302)
W. O. Henderson. *The Industrial Revolution in Europe.* (QP303)
Raul Hilberg. *The Destruction of the European Jews.* (QP301)
Richard N. Hunt. *German Social Democracy.* (QP306)
Telford Taylor. *Sword and Swastika.* (QP304)
John Weiss. *Nazis and Fascists in Europe, 1918-1945.* (NYTimes Book, QP305)

Philosophy

F. H. Bradley. *The Presuppositions of Critical History.* (QP108)
William Earle. *Objectivity.* (QP109)
James M. Edie, James P. Scanlan, Mary-Barbara Zeldin, George L. Kline. *Russian Philosophy.* (3 vols, QP111, 112, 113)
James M. Edie. *An Invitation to Phenomenology.* (QP103)
James M. Edie. *New Essays in Phenomenology.* (QP114)
James M. Edie. *Phenomenology in America.* (QP105)
R. O. Elveton. *The Phenomenology of Husserl.* (QP116)
Manfred S. Frings. *Heidegger and the Quest for Truth.* (QP107)
Moltke S. Gram. *Kant: Disputed Questions.* (QP104)
James F. Harris, Jr., and Richard Severens. *Analyticity.* (QP117)
E. D. Klemke. *Studies in the Philosophy of G. E. Moore.* (QP115)
Lionel Rubinoff. *Faith and Reason.* (QP106)
Stuart F. Spicker. *The Philosophy of the Body.* (QP118)
Paul Tibbetts. *Perception.* (QP110)
Pierre Thévenaz. *What Is Phenomenology?* (QP101)

Social Science

Shalom Endleman. *Violence in the Streets.* (QP215)
Nathan Glazer. *Cities in Trouble.* (NYTimes Book, QP212)
George and Eunice Grier. *Equality and Beyond.* (QP204)
Kurt Lang and Gladys Engel Lang. *Politics and Television.* (QP216)
Charles O. Lerche, Jr. *Last Chance in Europe.* (QP207)
Raymond W. Mack. *Prejudice and Race Relations.* (NYTimes Book, QP217)
David Mitrany. *A Working Peace System.* (QP205)
H. L. Nieburg. *In the Name of Science.* (QP218)
Martin Oppenheimer. *The Urban Guerrilla.* (QP219)
Martin Oppenheimer and George Lakey. *A Manual for Direct Action.* (QP202)
James Parkes. *Antisemitism.* (QP213)
Fred Powledge. *To Change a Child.* (QP209)
Lee Rainwater. *And the Poor Get Children.* (QP208)
The Rockefeller Report on the Americas. (QP214)
Clarence Senior. *The Puerto Ricans.* (QP201)
Harold L. Sheppard. *Poverty and Wealth in America.* (NYTimes Book, QP220)
Arthur L. Stinchcombe. *Rebellion in a High School.* (QP211)
Harry M. Trebing. *The Corporation in the American Economy.* (NYTimes Book, QP221)
David Manning White. *Pop Culture in America.* (NYTimes Book, QP222)